Organizing Foundations for Maximum Impact:
A Guide to Effective Philanthropy

Denis J. Prager

THE ASPEN INSTITUTE
Nonprofit Sector and Philanthropy Program

To purchase additional copies of this report, please contact:

The Aspen Institute
Publications Office
P.O. Box 222
109 Houghton Lab Lane
Queenstown, Maryland 21658
Phone: (410) 820-5433
Fax: (410) 827-9174
E-mail: publications@aspeninstitute.org

For all other inquiries, please contact:

The Aspen Institute
Nonprofit Sector and Philanthropy Program
One Dupont Circle, N.W.
Suite 700
Washington, DC 20036
Phone: (202) 736-5814
Fax: (202) 293-0525
Webpages: www.nonprofitresearch.org
          www.aspeninstitute.org

THE ASPEN] INSTITUTE

The Aspen Institute is an international nonprofit organization founded in 1950. Its mission is to foster enlightened leadership, the appreciation of timeless ideas and values, and open-minded dialogue on contemporary issues. Through seminars, policy programs, conferences and leadership development initiatives, the institute and its international partners seek to promote the pursuit of common ground and deeper understanding in a nonpartisan and nonideological setting. The Institute is headquartered in Washington, DC, and has campuses in Aspen, Colorado, and on the Wye River on Maryland's Eastern Shore. Its international network includes partner Aspen Institutes in Berlin, Rome, Lyon and Tokyo, and leadership programs in Africa. To learn more about the Institute or to sign up for one of its seminars, visit www.aspeninstitute.org.

Nonprofit Sector and Philanthropy Program

The Aspen Institute's Nonprofit Sector and Philanthropy Program (NSPP) seeks to improve the operation of the nonprofit sector and philanthropy through research and dialogue focused on public policy, management, and other important issues affecting the nonprofit sector. It includes the:

Nonprofit Sector Research Fund (NSRF): The Fund is a grantmaking entity that awards support to university-based and other researchers studying nonprofit activities. It also produces a variety of publications, including grant guidelines; an annual report; working papers based on Fund-supported research; Nonprofit Research News, a newsletter reporting on the Nonprofit Sector Research Fund's activities and research; and *Snapshots*, brief, easy-to-use bulletins summarizing key findings and practical studies supported by the Fund. The Fund also publishes an electronic newsletter, *The Philanthropy Information Retrieval Project* (PIRP), which reports on new ideas and other developments that may affect the field of philanthropy in the years to come.

Nonprofit Sector Strategy Group: The Strategy Group was a leadership forum that met from 1997-2001. The initiative convened top nonprofit, government, and business leaders to address the most pressing issues facing the nonprofit sector in America.

Kellogg-Kauffman Seminar Series for Mid-Continent Foundation CEOs:
The Kellogg-Kauffman Seminar brings together a small group of mid-continent foundation executives to discuss issues of mutual interest.

The State of America's Nonprofit Sector Project: This project is producing an important series of reference books assessing the condition of the nonprofit sector in the United States.

For more information about the Nonprofit Sector and Philanthropy Program's activities, visit www.aspeninstitute.org or www.nonprofitresearch.org.

The Aspen Institute
Nonprofit Sector and Philanthropy Program
One Dupont Circle, NW
Suite 700
Washington, DC 20036
(202) 736-5800

Table of Contents

Preface .... *vii*

Acknowledgments .... *ix*

I. PHILANTHROPY: OPPORTUNITIES AND DILEMMAS 1

Introduction 2

Chapter 1: Private Foundations:
The Institution and the Opportunity 3
    The Institution
    The Opportunity

Chapter 2: Giving Away Money is Easy. Isn't It? 5
    The Flip Side of Opportunity
    The Nature of the Beast
    Some Inherent Tensions, Contradictions

II. THE PRIZE AND HOW TO PURSUE IT SYSTEMATICALLY 15

Introduction 16

Chapter 3: The Prize and How to Keep Our Eye On It 17
    The Prize
    How to Keep Our Eye On It

Chapter 4: Pursuing the Prize Systematically 21
    In-Depth Knowledge of the Field and Its Levers of Change
    Systematic Deployment of Resources
    The Element of Time
    Intimate Involvement of Key Constituencies
    Mobilizing Communities to Address Their Own Problems
    Infrastructure Development
    The Role of Communications

Chapter 5: Self-Assessment: Measuring, Learning, Improving 35
    The Evaluation Conundrum
    Why Is It So Hard?
    The Case For Self-Assessment
    Guiding Principles

III. ORGANIZING FOR MAXIMUM IMPACT 43

Introduction *44*

Chapter 6: The Board is Where it All Starts *45*
    Introduction
    Board Roles and Responsibilities
    Principles of Good Governance
    Conduct and Behavior
    Building an Effective Board
    Maintaining an Effective Board

Chapter 7: Executive Management: Linking Policy and Action...*65*
    Key Link and Integrative Force
    Roles and Responsibilities
    Attributes of Effective Chief Executives

Chapter 8: The Staff: Getting the Job Done *73*
    The Front Line of Philanthropy
    Program Staff Roles and Responsibilities
    Conduct and Behavior
    Attributes of Effective Program Staff
    Enhancing and Sustaining Staff Effectiveness

Chapter 9: Organizing for Maximum Impact *89*
    Organization Matters
    Making the Organization Work

Epilogue...*95*

Appendix A: Board Conflict of Interest – Model Policy and
    Disclosure Form..*97*

Appendix B: Staff Conflict of Interest – Model Policy and
    Disclosure Form *103*

About the Author...*109*

Preface

L ate in 1997, Dr. Karen Feinstein, President of the Jewish Healthcare
Foundation of Pittsburgh, initiated a year-long series of discussions intended to lead to recommendations for increasing the capacity of foundations
to define their roles, design their programs, deploy their resources, and assess their
outcomes more strategically and effectively. Dr. Feinstein articulated her ultimate
goal as "raising the value of philanthropy."

As part of that effort, I was commissioned to write a paper on the characteristics
of foundation program and assessment strategies judged to be most effective. The
principal input to that paper was interviews with seventeen people from both
inside and outside the field of philanthropy. The resulting paper – *"Raising the
Value of Philanthropy: A Synthesis of Informal Interviews with Foundation Executives
and Observers of Philanthropy"* – was published by Grantmakers In Health (GIH)
in January of 1999.

The reception accorded the paper was extraordinary. GIH went through the initial
printing almost immediately, and has since distributed thousands of copies in
printed and electronic form. I continue to be contacted by people who have just
been given a copy of the paper and think it is insightful, constructive and helpful.
To an unexpected degree, the paper seems to feed a hunger among members of
foundation boards and staffs to learn about what works best in maximizing the
impact of philanthropy, especially from someone with extensive experience in the
field.

It's not that there hasn't been a great deal written over the years about philanthropy – its origins, history, distinctive role in American society, glories and perceived failures. It's just that most of this writing has been by people from outside
philanthropy, observers of social institutions who, by and large, believe that foundations are not living up to their potential to contribute to the solution of major
social problems. The rise in both the quantity and harshness of this criticism over
the last several decades seems to reflect: (i) the rapid growth in philanthropic
assets that resulted from the stock market boom in the late 1990's and early
2000's, and the establishment of a large number of new foundations; (ii) the rise
of political conservatism in this country and its distrust of what are perceived to
be socially liberal institutions; and (iii) widespread curiosity about these independent institutions and how they operate.

Criticism can help goad institutions do more and better. However, to be useful, it must be based on objective analyses of their strengths and weaknesses, in the context of a realistic assessment of what is possible given the environment in which they operate. What organized philanthropy needs most, at this point in its evolution, is not more invective, but serious efforts to make it better, by people who, while objective, understand philanthropy, what it can and cannot be expected to undertake, the operations of foundations, and what are emerging as proven best practices.

That, at least, is the premise of this volume. It is intended to capture and articulate, as coherently as possible: (i) the essence of effective philanthropy as carried out by organized foundations; (ii) the obligations and responsibilities of, and relationships among, foundation boards, executive managers and staff; (iii) how foundations should be organized for maximum effectiveness; and (iv) how foundations should relate to their principal partners and constituencies. However, it is hoped that what is written here will also be of interest to a wide range of "outsiders" – policy-makers, executive directors of nonprofit agencies, fundraisers, and anyone else interested in what philanthropy is all about, and how foundations operate.

Disclaimer: What follows is one man's opinion formed through eleven years developing and managing grantmaking programs in a large foundation, nine years consulting for a wide variety of clients, large and small, new and old, and interactions with a large number of extremely wise people both within and outside the field. However, in the end, it is still one man's opinion. There is no pretense of scholarship, rigor or comprehensiveness. Rather, it is an effort to collect, in one place, what I have learned from direct involvement, observation and listening about maximizing the effectiveness of foundations and their programs. It is expected that people in the field will disagree with things that are written here. I hope that such disagreements will catalyze more and better writing on the subject, and lead to efforts within the field to collect, share and apply what we know, as a community, to increasing the degree to which philanthropy lives up to its potential to contribute to improving the human condition.

Denis J. Prager, Ph.D.

June 2003

Acknowledgments

I t was Karen Feinstein who recognized the need to raise the value of philanthropy and provided the leadership and energy necessary to spearhead a process designed to figure out how to do it. Ultimately, it is she who is the mother of this monograph. Its midwives were the 17 people who spent so much time with me sharing their perspectives on the characteristics of effective philanthropy as practiced by organized foundations: Drew Altman; Doreen Boyce; Thomas David; Karen Davis; Judith Feder; Dan Fox; John Gardner (we do miss him so!); Charles Halpern; Paul Jellinek; Margaret Mahoney; Magda Peck; Kenneth Prewitt; Mark Smith; Karl Stauber; Vivien Stewart; Franklin Tugwell, and Marni Vliet. I can't thank them enough for their patience and wisdom.

Along the way, I have received a great deal of help and encouragement from a large number of people, including especially: Jessie Gruman (Center for the Advancement of Health); Gary Yates (California Wellness Foundation); Deborah Brody Hamilton (National Center for Family Philanthropy); and Ray Boyer (MacArthur Foundation). I also want to acknowledge and thank the many clients with whom I have worked over the last nine years for the opportunity to learn firsthand about philanthropy from an extraordinarily array of organizations and settings. And they thought that *I* was helping *them*!

I want to thank, especially, Alan Abramson, director of the Nonprofit Sector and Philanthropy Program at The Aspen Institute, for betting that the information contained in this monograph will be of general interest to both the philanthropic and nonprofit sectors, and Winnifred Levy, the Program's Manager of Communications, for her expert and patient guidance of this volume through the publication process.

Last, but certainly not least, I want to thank my wife, Barbara, for her unstinting love and support.

I.
Philanthropy: Opportunities and Dilemmas

Introduction

Much of this volume deals with strategies for organizing foundations in such a way as to maximize their operational effectiveness and efficiency, and their programmatic effectiveness and impact. However, before getting into the these more prosaic aspects of philanthropy, it is important to set the context for that work in terms of what foundations are, the opportunities they have to achieve important societal goals, the obligations inherent in those opportunities, and the dilemmas and tensions foundations face in carrying out their work. The principal myth this section aims to dispel is that giving money away is easy. With a firmer understanding of the challenges of effective philanthropy, we can dig deeper into the details of how effective philanthropy can best be achieved.

Chapter 1: Private Foundations: The Institution and the Opportunity

THE INSTITUTION

Foundations are nonprofit organizations that exist solely to improve the human condition. As such, they occupy a distinctive niche in our free enterprise economic system, through which the fruits of financial success can be partly returned to society in the form of philanthropic dollars.

The power of philanthropy stems largely from the fact that foundations have:

Great Independence – Compared with most other institutions in our society, foundations are afforded an extraordinary level of independence and freedom from regulation and oversight. The protected legal status and financial resources of foundations combine to free them from the need to accede to pressures brought by voters, stockholders, or contributors, and to give them extraordinary power and opportunity to advance the public good.

A Long Time Horizon – Because, in contrast to government, business, and other non-profit organizations, foundations are permitted to manage their resources to last in perpetuity, they can take a long-term view of the societal problems they tackle and their role in addressing them. Foundations that exploit this long time horizon have the potential to look ahead, anticipate changing forces and influences, adopt appropriate funding strategies, and stick with those strategies until they bear fruit. In philanthropy, time pressures are largely self-imposed and usually not productive (more about this later).

Neutral Standing – As a function of their privileged and protected status and independence, foundations are perceived to be neutral, objective, and credible forces for good within the communities they serve. If used effectively, this standing gives foundations significant power and leverage to mobilize the resources, leadership, and talent needed to address the large number of complex, interacting problems that characterize society.

THE OPPORTUNITY

Foundations have an extraordinary opportunity to contribute to the health and well-being of the people they serve. No matter the size of its assets, the nature of its legacy, the focus of its grantmaking, or the scope of its activities, every foundation has the potential to make a real difference in the lives of individuals, families, and communities.

For board members and staff, serving a foundation is like nothing else they will ever do: the money is in the bank; their only obligation is to protect and spend it wisely; the goal is to advance the human condition; and the horizon is forever! What an opportunity they have to:

Serve the Community – Using the foundation's full set of resources (as we'll see later, money is only one asset) to help meet the needs of people. Where else can an individual put his or her talents to work in directing protected assets to solving the kinds of social problems they see around them every day?

Lead, Shape, Manage, or Operate an Organization Intended to Last in Perpetuity – With most foundations, the intent is that the money will be invested and spent in such a way that financial resources will be available to contribute to the community forever. Board and staff members are really stewards of a foundation's legacy and assets, which are entrusted to them to manage and distribute prudently and wisely.

Grow and Learn – Serving as board or staff of a foundation represents an extraordinary chance for personal growth and intellectual stretching, and for learning about areas of human endeavor to which they've never been exposed. For both, informed decision-making is an imperative, not a luxury, and the learning necessary for informed decisions means personal growth of a kind seldom experienced in other domains of their lives.

But, as we hear all too often, there is no free lunch and no good deed goes unpunished. With these truisms in mind, let's look at the obligations and responsibilities that one assumes when serving a foundation as board or staff.

Chapter 2: Giving away Money is Easy. Isn't It?

THE FLIP SIDE OF OPPORTUNITY

The extraordinary opportunities described in Chapter 1 are more than matched by the obligations and hard work entailed in being an effective member of a foundation's board or staff. Much of this monograph deals with the obligations they bear as they grapple with how best to fulfill their special roles and responsibilities. This chapter focuses on the part about hard work.

Hard work? Isn't giving away money easy? How hard can it be to hand out money to well-meaning organizations doing worthwhile things? That's the question going through people's minds when they learn that you are on the board or staff of a foundation. If they're old enough, they remember the TV show called "The Millionaire," in which the star handed out money to supposedly deserving individuals. If they're younger, they immediately think about an organization with which they or a relative is involved – a church, soup kitchen, shelter, local health clinic, environmental advocacy organization, etc. – and figure that giving money to such worthy organizations must be easy.

In fact, giving away money *is* easy. But giving money away the *right* way is very, very difficult. In fact, even knowing what we mean by "right" is problematic. Let's take a look at some of the factors that make effective philanthropy a challenge.

The Complexity of the Problems: Foundations exist to contribute to improving the human condition, whether it be by improving the health and well-being of individuals; strengthening families and communities; protecting the environment and natural resources; improving international relations and reducing the threat of war; or supporting economic development in the Third World. By their very nature, however, these kinds of societal challenges are extremely complex, involving the behaviors of individuals, social systems, and political processes; their underlying causes may encompass everything from genes to the environment; and their roots are often deep-seated, long-standing, and difficult to elucidate, much less change.

5

Resource Limitations: No matter how rich the foundation, its resources are meager compared with the magnitude of the societal problems it exists to help solve. In most cases, only governments have the kinds of resources required to address the kinds of complex problems mentioned above. As we will see later on, *the critical challenge facing foundations is using their resources in a focused and strategic way to identify and engage social issues with highly targeted efforts and maximum leverage.*

Assessing Outcomes: Foundations strive to make a difference in some specific aspect of the lives of people in the communities they serve. Yet, perhaps the most significant challenge they face is knowing if their programs are fulfilling their missions. First, there is the difficulty of even defining exactly what a programmatic goal should be. For example, should it be to reduce the number of births to unwed teens in a community, or to increase the number of young women served by community-based programs? While setting quantitative goals for ultimate outcomes is attractive from programmatic and accountability perspectives, doing so may not be realistic, given the complexity of the social processes involved. Second, it is extremely difficult to demonstrate that the foundation's efforts had an impact. Not only are reliable and timely data hard to come by, but once a change is discerned, it is even harder to attribute that change to the foundation's actions. In fact, it may well be that despite the foundation's best efforts, the change measured was in the wrong direction. Returning to our example, while the number of unwed teens reached by the agencies supported by the foundation increased significantly, the number of out-of-wedlock births to those women may have also increased, due to economic forces, requirements of entitlement programs, or other secular trends completely out of the foundation's control.

Reinventing the Wheel: There is little accumulated knowledge in the field of philanthropy about what works and what doesn't. The tremendous experience gathered over the decades by thousands of foundations struggling to effect social change is not readily accessible to those grappling with the same problems today. Important efforts are being made by organizations like the Council on Foundations, the Foundation Center, various "affinity groups" of foundations with shared goals and interests, and even some foundations; and, modern communications technologies such as the World Wide Web are certainly facilitating increased access to information and people. Yet there are still no effective central resources to which foundation board members and staff can turn to learn about the experiences of others in maximizing the effectiveness of philanthropy in addressing specific social challenges. As a result, instead of learning from those who have gone before them and perhaps replicating their successes and avoiding their failures, foundations constantly reinvent the wheel, squandering precious money, time, and energy.

Partnering: Given the immensity of the social challenges foundations exist to meet, the limited resources they bring to the table, and the nature of their principal modus operandi – grantmaking – it is a practical necessity that most foundations form partnerships with others pursuing similar goals – grantees, other foundations, and government agencies. Yet true partnerships are extremely difficult to create and sustain. By "true," I mean relationships in which the partners share goals, outcome indicators, approaches, responsibility, and, in some cases, funding. True partnerships with grantees are illusory, because of the imbalance of power that is inherent in a relationship in which one party has resources that the other covets. True partnerships among foundations exist more in rhetoric than reality, due mostly to the independence and differing operational styles and time-lines that characterize these institutions. And true partnerships between foundations and governments are rare as a result of their vastly different organizational structures, decision-making processes and time frames, susceptibility to external pressures, and the suspicion with which they sometimes view each other.

THE NATURE OF THE BEAST

By its very nature, the world of philanthropy is idiosyncratic and decentralized. Or, as is commonly heard among observers of the field, "if you've seen one foundation, you've seen one foundation!" One need only peruse foundation annual reports and study the results of the annual surveys conducted by the Council of Foundations (www.cof.org) to recognize the tremendous diversity among foundations, in terms of the source and magnitude of resources, board composition, staff size, substantive focus, organizational structure, management style, and grantmaking approach.

The remarkable independence afforded foundations as a result of their legal status and endowments makes it possible for them to set aside considerations of popularity or profitability and move beyond pre-existing agendas to promote social progress as they define it. While this lack of clear external accountability is one of philanthropy's major assets, it is also one of its greatest weaknesses. Unlike most other institutions, there are no commonly accepted standards against which to measure the effectiveness and impact of foundations. This lack of benchmarks and performance criteria is exacerbated by the fact that many foundations believe their mission to be changing social conditions and institutions in such a way as to bring about major improvements in people's lives – an outcome that is not easily measurable.

A major implication of the independence, diversity, and decentralization of the field of philanthropy is that while it may be possible and useful to develop model guidelines, standards, performance criteria, and assessment strategies for the field, each foundation will have to adapt them to suit its particular situation. What foundations do, how they do it, and how they assess their impacts are all influenced by the origins of their assets, their missions, the composition of their boards, their geographic purview, and the environments in which they operate.

SOME INHERENT TENSIONS, CONTRADICTIONS

Before presenting some characteristics of effective philanthropy and discussing the special roles and responsibilities of foundation boards, leaders, and staffs, it may be useful to at least touch on some of the tensions and contradictions that are inherent in grantmaking and in the organizational strategies through which foundations attempt to carry out their missions – further evidence that giving away money the right way is not easy.

Proactive vs. Responsive Grant Making: Over the last decade, there has been a growing trend among foundations to decide how to attack the social problems that constitute their mandates, design and generate initiatives for addressing them, and invite organizations to submit proposals for support. This approach is referred to as proactive, strategic, or initiative grant making, as contrasted with responsive grant making, the more traditional strategy in which grants are awarded in response to unsolicited proposals. From the perspective of some foundation boards and staffs, proactive grant making is a way for a foundation to deploy its resources in a coherent, comprehensive, and integrated manner to address complex social problems. From the perspective of prospective grantees, however, such grant making seems to be yet another attempt to "raise the bar" over which organizations must jump to receive the support they need to sustain their operations. These organizations resent what appears to be arrogance on the part of foundation staff who, through their use of strategic initiatives, seem to be saying, "We know best how to solve the problems on which you are working every day."

With the passage of time, and the growth of experience with different approaches to grantmaking, a consensus appears to be emerging that the most effective grant making programs are those that comprise a mix of strategic initiatives, responsive grant making, and discretionary funds set aside for targets of opportunity. Foundations initially enamored with strategic approaches have come to appreciate the value of responding to ideas proposed by organizations "in the trenches and on the ground," grappling with the realities of social change on a daily basis, while those funding solely through responsive mechanisms have come to recognize the advantages of strategic initiatives in permitting more focused, integrated efforts to effect change.

Innovation vs. General Operating Support: Paralleling the trend toward proactive grant making has been the growing tendency for foundations to fund programs they consider to be innovative, creative, and imaginative, rather than those seeking support for ongoing operations. In part, this represents frustration with the seeming ineffectiveness of existing approaches to complex social problems, and with the organizations employing them. In part, it is the natural tendency of boards and staff to want to be associated with something new, different, and exciting. The danger, in the eyes of some, is that foundations may pursue innovation for the sake of innovation – or, as some see it, difference for the sake of difference – when providing support for what has already been shown to work may, in fact, be the best approach.

This love affair with innovation has significant consequences for the grant-seeking community. First, it forces organizations desperately in need of support for ongoing operations to invent projects that appear to fulfill a foundation's criteria for creativity. While doing so may help the organization reach new levels of effectiveness, it may actually distort and diffuse its mission, further stretch its resources, and dilute its effectiveness. Second, it puts organizations that receive support for specific projects in the position of having to: demonstrate the effectiveness of those projects, rather than the organization's overall impact; collect data they might not otherwise collect; and prove that their projects were responsible for the changes measured. Third, organizations whose administrative structures are already stretched, must now account separately for expenses associated with new projects. What's worse, in the eyes of some, is that organizations desperate for funding to support their core programs and operations may be forced to be as creative in writing proposals and in reporting on expenditures, activities, and outcomes as they are in the carrying out their programs.

Again, what appears to be emerging is an approach that combines the best features of each of these approaches: (i) targeted project support for the development and demonstration of innovative projects designed to take organizations and their programs to the next level; and (ii) general support for organizations with proven track records in operating programs that make a difference in areas of central interest to the foundation.

Grants as Charitable Donations vs. Grants as Investments: The drive to catalyze innovation in addressing social ills, coupled with the move to a more proactive approach to grant making, has led some foundations to apply venture capital strategies to their grants programs. This is true, especially, among the new foundations established by entrepreneurs whose success in the "new economy" has made them wealthy. To them, it is only natural to apply to philanthropy the practices that made them successful entrepreneurs – a strong emphasis on return on investment; the setting of goals with measurable outcomes (the "bottom line"); active involvement in the organizations being supported; and insistence on sound financial practices. Underlying the new "venture philanthropy" strategies is the view of foundation grants as investments in the programs and organizations being supported, rather than the more traditional view (and legal definition) of grants as charitable donations. This shift in perspective has important implications for how foundations define their goals, determine which implementation strategies to employ, select grantees, relate to those grantees, and measure the progress of funded projects. It also affects the kinds of people they hire to become program officers and how those officers divide their time between developing programs and assisting existing programs.

While the venture capital approach to grant making has been adopted by some foundations, its suitability and appropriateness as a model for philanthropy is being widely debated both within and outside the field. Balancing the view that foundations should be more concerned with the return they receive on the investments they make is the view that, in the end, foundations achieve their goals by identifying and supporting good people and good organizations carrying out successful programs, and providing the resources they need to carry out their work most effectively.

Social Change vs. Service Delivery: Another tension in philanthropy is between supporting organizations providing services aimed at helping people in immediate need, and funding organizations attempting to catalyze long-term social change so that the need for those services is reduced. An example is the choice between providing support for a center for battered women, helping it increase the number of women it can serve, or supporting the development and implementation of public policies and programs aimed at reducing the number of women in need of services by preventing abuse before it leads to violence. Sometimes the contrast is characterized as eliminating the root causes of social ills rather than treating the symptoms. However it is conceptualized, it is the focus of intense debate both within and outside philanthropy.

On the one hand, a strong case can be made for foundations being the only social institutions with the financial and political independence and perspective necessary to mobilize the resources and to bring about social change. And, it is highly satisfying to be participating in activities that have the potential to make an enduring difference in the lives of people for generations. On the other hand, a strong case can be made for the humanitarian imperative of protecting and enhancing the well being of those in need now. And it is much easier to quantify and measure services delivered and people helped than it is to assess and attribute the contribution of a foundation to bringing about changes in complex social systems and structures.

Demonstrating Impacts vs. Contributing to the Process: Related to the growing demand for greater accountability in philanthropy is the increasing attention being paid to program assessment and evaluation. Talk among foundations these days is all about outcomes and how to measure them. This move toward demonstrating program impact is not only understandable, but is an indication of the seriousness with which foundation boards are taking their fiduciary responsibilities. However, there is the danger that the preoccupation with measurable outcomes and objective evidence may prevent foundations from tackling the kinds of big issues they are so well positioned to address, and from taking the kinds of risks that only they can take.

Further, foundations may be misleading themselves and others by attempting to apply rigorous scientific evaluation to areas that, by their very nature, are multi-dimensional, ambiguous, and changing. The fact is that the large number of complex, interacting factors acting on any social process makes it extremely difficult to demonstrate the singular contribution of a foundation program to a change in that process. Thus, if foundations fund only those programs that lend themselves to quantitative evaluation, they may be limiting their purview to problems with limited scope and programs with narrow objectives. If the search for quantitative bench-marking of programs is taken too far, foundations will end up focusing their attention on things that are most measurable rather than those that are most important. It's analogous, in a way, to limiting the search for those proverbial lost keys to the area under the lamppost.

Considerations such as these, along with the growing disenchantment and disappointment with traditional "hard hat" evaluation methods, are leading many foundations to reassess their approaches to demonstrating program impact. What is emerging from these self-reflections is a growing conceptualization of *philanthropy as a continuous learning process in which foundations and their grantee organizations partner in the development, testing, refinement, and adoption of new strategies for improving the lives of those living in the communities they serve.* (You'll learn more about this later)

Production vs. Learning: A more internal, organizational tension is between the imperative to develop, prepare, and award grants to meet payout requirements, and the oft-stated, but less often realized, desire to nurture, monitor, assess, and learn from funded projects. This tension might be characterized as between the production side of grant making – getting the money out the door – and the learning side of grant making – gaining knowledge from the experience of grantees about what works and what doesn't, and using that knowledge to improve the effectiveness of grantees, to enhance foundation programs, and to advance the particular field of interest. Many see this learning function of foundations as the most important element of what they do; yet few have figured out how to avoid having the important crowded out by the immediate.

In part, this situation reflects the tyranny of the grant cycle; in part, it reflects the reward structures within foundations. It is a fact of life that, in the real world of grant making, the grant cycle (proposal processing, due diligence on applicants, preparation of compelling write-ups for the board, and the awarding of grants) becomes the predominant force driving the work of the staff, absorbing most of their time and energy, and leaving little for the learning part of their jobs. In most foundation settings, staffers barely have time following each board meeting for a collective sigh of relief before they must launch directly into the next round of proposals. Unfortunately, this often means that monitoring ongoing grants, reading reports, visiting grantees, and reflecting on their experiences is something staff dream about and plan for, but seldom get to.

Further, there are few incentives for staff to devote their time to assessing, learning from, or reflecting on, funded programs. Given the difficulty of evaluating the effectiveness of grantees and their programs and the impact of the foundation's grant making initiatives, it is easier to judge and reward staff on the production of paper products and their adherence to the deadlines inherent in the grant cycle. Thus, a premium is placed on pleasing the board by providing them with high-quality proposal justifications and optimistic and "rosy" reports on ongoing programs, and the reward structures in most foundations favor the completion of elements of the internal grants process rather than the achievement of desired program outcomes.

II.

The Prize and How to Pursue it Systematically

Introduction

Despite the challenges and dilemmas that make it so difficult to give money away the right way, there are conceptual frameworks, strategies, and practices gleaned from experience that, if adhered to, increase the effectiveness of philanthropy. This section summarizes what many leaders and observers of the field of philanthropy believe are some of the most critical elements of successful foundation programs. First, it focuses on the driving purpose and intent behind a foundation's decision to launch a new programmatic initiative – *The Prize*. Second, it emphasizes the importance of pursuing *The Prize* in a systematic fashion. Third, it stresses the imperative of involving all relevant constituent communities, from beginning to end, in programs in which they have a vested interest. Fourth, it stresses the critical role of time in effective foundation programs.

Chapter 3: The Prize and How to Keep Your Eye on it

THE PRIZE

We often say "keep your eye on the prize" when emphasizing how important it is to have a single-minded focus on the goal one is striving to achieve. The phrase connotes a strong sense of purpose and intensity of effort required to make something happen.

The same is true for foundations. For a foundation, *The Prize* is its raison d'e-tre – the mission it exists to pursue, the programmatic goals it strives to attain, and the outcomes for which it holds itself accountable. Conceptually, *The Prize* drives everything a foundation does and how it does it – governance, leadership philosophy, organizational structure, operational style, program-matic strategy, and staffing. Practically, *The Prize* is: (i) the banner behind which everyone marches, bringing the board, staff, grantees, and other part-ners together in a common, shared effort to effect a change they all agree is a worthy objective; (ii) the rationale behind the efforts of these partners to bring resources, energy, and talent in a concerted effort to achieve a specific outcome; (iii) the glue that binds different projects, grantees, and activities into a coherent, integrated whole aimed at the same ultimate outcome; and (iv) the basis on which the foundation measures its performance, learns about what works and what doesn't, and adapts its efforts accordingly.

HOW TO KEEP OUR EYE ON IT

Sustained Concentration: If *The Prize* represents a foundation's raison d'etre, collective vision, and driving force, it follows that a critical element in the foundation's success is the degree to which the board and staff keep their eye on it in a consistent and sustained way. Success in philanthropy, as in other endeavors, favors those who: (i) are absolutely clear about what they are working toward; (ii) maintain their focus on that goal and hold themselves accountable for reaching it; (iii) mobilize their resources to pursue the goal single-mindedly; and (iv) organize themselves for maximum effectiveness and efficiency.

Too often, however, foundation boards and staffs take their eyes off *The Prize*, becoming isolated from the world in which they operate, forgetting what it is they are trying to achieve, *overall*, failing to stick with focuses long enough to have an impact, and increasingly focusing on internal concepts, processes, and bureaucratic procedures, at the expense of external ideas, experiences, and realities. They launch new programs with goals clearly in mind and strategies for achieving them clearly in place. However, in time, goals often become diffuse and strategies fragmented. This loss of concentration is the result of several forces at work in philanthropy. These include:

Dilution of Focus and Resources – All foundations, no matter the magnitude of their assets or the narrowness of their purview, are faced with a daunting array of societal ills toward which they can direct their resources. Since each of those ills has potentially serious consequences for the lives of individuals and families, and the communities in which they live, deciding among them is often wrenching. As a result, foundations too often spread their resources across many problem areas, rather than making the kinds of tough decisions it takes to focus intensively on a small number where they can make the greatest difference.

Demands of the Market Place – In reality, there are many more meritorious ideas and worthy organizations in an area than any foundation has the resources to support. And given the realities of the nonprofit world, many of those ideas may languish and organizations perish without funding from private foundations. As a result, foundations feel great pressure to say "yes" to proposals, even when saying "no" is more consistent with their singular focus and strategic plan. This is particularly true for community-based foundations, where board and staff are in close contact with the issues, problems, and needs of their communities, and with the individuals and organizations struggling to address them.

Institutional Drift – In time, organizations tend to become preoccupied with form – internal politics, policies, procedures, and structures – at the expense of substance – *The Prize* and how best to attain it. This is true for foundations, too. Here, a number of factors lead to a gradual erosion of the initial flush of excitement, singular focus, intensity, and optimism surrounding the initiation of new programs. Among the factors at work are: (i) the requirement to meet annual distribution targets; (ii) the pressure of grant cycle and board meeting deadlines; (iii) the difficult challenge of having an impact on almost any social problem identified as a focus of a foundation's grantmaking; (iv) the even greater difficulty of demonstrating that the foundation's efforts actually made a difference; (v) the problem of knowing how to assess the performance of staff vis-á-vis program effectiveness and outcomes; and (vi) the tendency of board and, sometimes staff, to become bored with a program area and enthralled with new ones ("donor fatigue").

Coherent Sense of Purpose: Foundations that seem to do the best job of keeping their eyes on *The Prize* are those best able to sustain a coherent sense of who they are, what they are trying to accomplish, and how they are trying to accomplish it. Real effectiveness in philanthropy derives from a pervading sense of institutional coherence. This sense manifests itself as a consistent conceptual and operational framework that the foundation uses to: (i) determine its focus and priorities; (ii) make decisions about which opportunities to pursue; (iii) establish its implementation strategies; and (iv) control the natural tendency to branch out into too many areas. Such institutional coherence serves not only as the internal beacon that guides everything the foundation does, but also as a sign to the outside world of a consistency of purpose that brings credibility to the foundation's intentions and programs.

It is not always clear why foundations are doing what they are doing. In launching programs, foundations often fail to acknowledge the rationale underlying them and the outcomes they are intended to achieve. Lacking a clear articulation of their expectations, foundations then have no basis for accountability, finding it difficult, if not impossible, to evaluate their impacts and to demonstrate that they have made effective use of the resources at their command. In contrast, effective foundations continually reexamine the purposes of philanthropy, and constantly assess the degree to which the programs they fund are consistent with their missions, values, and principles. In selecting their priorities and designing their programs, these foundations ask: How do we add optimum value with the resources available to the foundation? What are the foundation's comparative advantages in addressing the particular issue or problem? What are the fundamental values and principles to which we must adhere as we move forward? And, how will we know if we are meeting our own expectations?

Focus: The more disciplined and focused the work of a foundation, the more likely it is to have an impact. No matter the size of its assets and the level of its annual payout, the resources available to a foundation pale in comparison to the magnitude of the social problems it exists to address. Accordingly, effective foundations are perceived to be those that focus their attention and their resources on a relatively small number of social problems, issues, or needs that are consistent with their missions, perceived comparative advantages, and capacities to make a discernable difference.

There is a natural tendency among foundations gradually to expand their purviews in an attempt to mitigate the many social problems that exist in the communities they serve, and to respond to the importunings of organizations struggling to address those problems. Ultimately, however, the resulting diffusion of emphasis serves to: (i) dilute the capacity of foundations to have a significant impact in any one area; (ii) reduce the effectiveness of boards in overseeing their foundations' programs and assessing their outcomes; (iii) reduce the ability of staffs to develop, facilitate, monitor and evaluate programs; and (iv) confuse the external world.

The most effective foundations are those that are able to resist this temptation to "be all things to all people" and to sustain a focus of attention and action that is driven by a coherent and consistent sense of values, principles, mission, and comparative advantages.

Chapter 4: Pursuing the Prize Systematically

Having defined *The Prize* it intends to pursue, the next challenge for a foundation is to establish a programmatic strategy and operational style that is most likely to achieve the goals it has set for itself. As stated earlier, the societal issues foundations exist to help solve are, by their very nature, complex, and deeply seated in social, cultural, and economic systems that defy easy solutions. *Accordingly, a fundamental thesis of this monograph is that a foundation's success in devising solutions to social problems lies in its ability to address them systematically.*

Being systematic implies matching a foundation's programmatic activities in a specific area to the goals they are intended to achieve, to the realities of the conditions in the field, and to the availability and readiness of people and institutions to make significant contributions to addressing the problem. As a function of their independence and resources, foundations represent the societal institution best able to recognize a significant social need, identify all the forces affecting that need, and systematically mobilize the full range of resources required to address the need in a comprehensive and sustained way. If foundations can't to this, who can? If foundations *don't* do this, why do we need them?

Acting systematically means designing foundation programs in such a way that their individual components represent elements of a coherent, integrated strategy intended not only to fill specific gaps, overcome specific barriers, and exploit specific opportunities, but to add up to something that, as a whole, contributes to making a difference in people's lives. Development and implementation of such strategies requires:

Thorough Knowledge of the Field – Basing action on an in-depth knowledge of the issue/problem/need being addressed;

Clear Theory of Change – Selecting an implementation strategy on the basis of a clearly articulated change theory and process judged to be the most effective one for achieving intended outcomes;

Strategic Deployment of Resources – Mobilizing and deploying all the resources available to the foundation in such a way as to increase the likelihood of success, and to attract and leverage the participation and resources of other partners;

Timeliness and Duration – Maximizing the potential for success by taking into account the realities of the environment in which the program will be operating and the readiness of actors to act, and sticking with a program for sufficient time to make a real difference;

Interaction With Key Constituencies – Involving key constituencies from the initial conceptualization through implementation to evaluation;

Mobilization of Communities – Strengthening the capacity of communities to solve their own problems; and

Communications – Including communication strategies and tools as integral elements of every program undertaken.

IN-DEPTH KNOWLEDGE OF THE FIELD AND ITS LEVERS OF CHANGE

Know the Field: Effective philanthropic programs are perceived to be those that are based on in-depth knowledge of the problem area in which a foundation intends to launch a program. A principal benefit of focusing attention and resources on a limited number of problems is the opportunity it gives a foundation to design and implement programs based on an intimate knowledge of those problems and of the environments in which they exist. More specifically, knowing a problem area intimately increases a foundation's ability to: (i) be more timely, opportunistic, and flexible in pursuit of program goals; (ii) understand how to manipulate the full range of factors involved in creating change; (iii) assess the potential effectiveness of alternative change strategies; (iv) respond knowledgeably to ideas proposed by others; and (v) feel comfortable with a messy change process that may require a fair amount of wallowing and groping before a clear path forward is identified.

Knowing the field means developing a feel for the big picture – the landscape and texture of the environment in which a problem is imbedded – as well as for the details of the problem, of the strategies best suited to addressing it, and of the degree to which the time is right for intervention. Developing this level of knowledge and familiarity starts with a willingness on the part of the foundation's board and staff to devote the time and energy necessary to become familiar with relevant literature concerning the problem, the environment in which it exists, and the experiences of others in attempting to address it, and to listening to people from a diversity of perspectives and interests capable of helping understand the problem and how it might best be addressed.

Identify Key Levers of Change: An important factor contributing to a foundation's effectiveness is a clear sense among board and staff of their theory of change. Systematic program implementation is likely to be more effective, and assessment of its impacts more meaningful, if it is based on a clear, rational, and conscious process of deciding which actions are most likely to achieve the desired change. Accordingly, it is important that a foundation include in its program development process, a separate and discrete step devoted to identifying the points of leverage where, if pressure is applied in a systematic and coherent way, change is effected. Before it can identify those points of leverage, a foundation must first understand the *entire* system within which a particular social problem is embedded, the targets of intervention that are likely to be most productive in addressing the problem, and the sequence of actions that have to be taken in order to achieve the desired change.

SYSTEMATIC DEPLOYMENT OF RESOURCES

There is a growing consensus among those working in the field of philanthropy that the effectiveness of a foundation program is directly related to the degree to which it is implemented systematically. Thus, once a foundation has determined its focus and goals, established a firm grounding of knowledge and understanding of the problem to be addressed, and selected a change process on which to base its programs, the next critical step is to determine how best to deploy its resources so that it achieves the most bang for the grantmaking buck.

Systematically Deploying *All* Available Resources: Beyond their financial assets, foundations have at their disposal a wide range of resources that, when deployed in a strategic fashion, have the potential to be much more powerful in addressing social problems than money alone. These include: (i) legal, structural, and financial independence; (ii) a singular focus on improving the human condition; (iii) neutrality; (iv) flexibility; (v) a long-term horizon; and (vi) the knowledge, experience, and skills of the board and staff. While grants represent the core of a foundation's strategy for achieving its programmatic goals, other elements of such a strategy include:

Convening – pulling together organizations and individuals that cut across the range of perspectives and capacities that must be mobilized if social problems are to be successfully addressed;

Leadership – serving as a catalyst in mobilizing community resources;

Technical Assistance – providing help in building the capacity of partner organizations to fulfill their missions more effectively; and

Communication and Education – raising the level of awareness and knowledge about the importance of a societal issue and how best to address it among the public, opinion leaders, and public officials.

Remaining Flexible: Effective foundations sustain a high level of flexibility in implementing their programs. A paradox in philanthropy is that, despite the freedom they have to establish their own program goals and implementation schedules, foundations often become just as bureaucratic and rigid as other societal institutions. Often, the conventions of traditional grant processes force foundations to be more restrictive and prescriptive about the requirements of their grants than is appropriate for programs operating in the real world.

Given the rapid rate at which change takes place in the social, economic, and political environments in which foundations operate, there is a growing need for them to allocate resources in such a way as to adapt to that change and take advantage of emerging and unanticipated opportunities. In practice, this may involve:

- Anticipating, and being explicit about, the milieu in which a foundation program will be operating, including the limitations and barriers it faces;

- Assuring that the expectations of the board, staff, grantees, and other constituencies are realistic;

- Helping the foundation board become comfortable with the risks inherent in operating in fluid environments;

- Modifying program strategies in response to changing realities, including the jettisoning of initiatives that no longer make sense; and

- Shifting resources to exploit new opportunities within the foundation's mission.

THE ELEMENT OF TIME

A critical element contributing to the success of foundation efforts to improve social conditions is time – the degree to which the time is right to launch an initiative (timing); the way in which the various elements of the initiative are phased in (staging); and the length of the foundation's commitment (duration).

Timing: People who have been in the field of philanthropy a long time come to understand the critical contribution of timing to the eventual success of a program. We often talk about someone who had the right idea at the right time, with the implication that the timing was simply fortuitous. However, in the development and launching of foundation programs, timing need not be a hit-or-miss matter. A critical element in selecting the focus for a foundation initiative and in designing an intervention strategy appropriate for that focus, is determining the degree to which the environment is ready for, and receptive to, change. If the time is right and the environment is receptive, a foundation's initiative may be like throwing a match on dry tinder; if it is not, even the most creative strategy may fail to spark a response.

The Natural History of Program Initiatives: A major factor in the design and implementation of effective foundation programs is an understanding of the natural course of initiatives aimed at social improvement, and of the relationships on which those initiatives are based. Every effort to achieve change in a social condition goes through stages of development from early preparation of the environment in which the effort is to take place, through implementation of the change strategy, to preparation of the environment for withdrawal of foundation funding and activity. Failure to recognize this natural history of program initiatives, launching them, instead, on an arbitrary timetable determined by foundation funding cycles, may lead to implementation schedules that are inconsistent with real-world time frames, expectations that are unrealistic, and relationships that are unnecessarily strained and frustrating.

Getting Started Phase: Getting off to the right start is critical to the eventual success of a foundation initiative. The zeal to launch a new program, together with the imperative to move on to other projects and prepare for the next board meeting, often lead foundation staff to allow too little time to lay the groundwork for a new initiative. Doing so effectively involves:

- Making sure that the foundation's vision is shared by key participants, using their feedback to refine the vision and the strategy through which it is to be implemented;

- Preparing the environment so that, when it is time to launch the initiative, the way has been paved and all the necessary pieces are in place, using planning and development grants, as appropriate, to help critical organizations prepare to be active players; and

- Being prepared to go back to the drawing board to redesign an initiative, delaying it until the time is right, or scrapping it entirely if it appears likely to be ill-fated.

Implementation Phase: Effective foundation programs are characterized by pragmatism and realism in terms of what it takes to get things done. The implementation strategies they employ are interactive and iterative, recognizing that their first fix on a problem is likely to be so imprecise that they should not become wedded to it. Like any individual or organization trying to accomplish something significant, foundations have to allow for falls and bumps, make corrections and try again. This requires that they build into their implementation strategies opportunities to stop, take stock, and learn, to make mid-course corrections when necessary, and to cut losses when things aren't going well.

Assessment Phase: Consistent with this interactive, evolutionary view of effective program development and implementation, program assessment is not, as traditionally practiced, a separate and distinct activity instituted at the end of a program to determine its success. Rather, it is an ongoing learning strategy begun at the program's inception and sustained throughout its existence. More about this later.

Follow Up Phase: One of the weaknesses of many foundation programs is the failure to build into the programs the requisite time and resources needed to undertake the kind of follow up necessary to leave a lasting legacy. Elements of effective program follow up include:

- Assuring that effective interventions are institutionalized ("sustainability"). In the traditional model of foundation action, it was assumed that the role of the foundation was innovation. However, it is important that foundations anticipate what it will take for successful interventions to be institutionalized so that their impacts are sustained.

- Catalyzing the wider application of interventions that work ("going to scale"). Too often, effective social interventions are not replicated in such a way as to test their effectiveness in other settings, or to promote their wider acceptance and application in other communities and situations (innovation without scale-up). Or, in some instances, interventions are enacted by other communities or organizations before their effectiveness and wider applicability have been demonstrated (scale-up without innovation). If it is indeed less likely now that the government will assume responsibility for funding the replication and dissemination of effective new interventions, then it will be up to the foundations themselves to help figure out how to take them to scale. In this view of the world, it just doesn't make sense for foundations to invest in the development and testing of new interventions if they are not going to be willing to invest in the wider application of those that prove to be highly effective.

- Communicating the results of programs. A complaint heard by foundations struggling to address difficult social problems is that they are constantly re-inventing the wheel. The same forces that mitigate against foundations following up their successes also mitigate against their investing the time and resources necessary to capture what they have learned from a particular programmatic initiative – both successes and failures – and to share that information with other funders, as well as with other interested parties.

Exit Phase: How a foundation exits a program may be almost as important as how it enters it. Yet in many cases, this is the most neglected part of a foundation's program effort. When a foundation creates a new program, it creates a culture of relationships and interdependence in which the foundation plays a central role. Developing a conscious and deliberate strategy for withdrawing from that culture so that its partners are protected is not only a responsible way for a foundation to act, but also helps assure that the work it initiated is carried on. Accordingly, in establishing new program initiatives, it is important that foundations: (i) be absolutely clear in advance about how long they intend to fund a program; (ii) include in their initial program planning development of a deliberate exit strategy; and (iii) consciously manage the transition out of an initiative in such a way as to minimize its impact on grantees and other participants.

Duration: Foundations are often criticized for their failure to stick with programs long enough to make a significant difference. Due to the natural tendency on the part of boards and staffs to lose interest in what comes to be seen as the same old thing, to grow impatient with programs that take a long time to mature and produce results, and to want to be associated with initiatives that are new and exciting, foundations often terminate initiatives before they have had sufficient time to pay off. Unfortunately, achieving significant results in efforts to bring about social improvements takes time. To be effective in such efforts, foundations need to: (i) adopt a longer time perspective when deciding to address important social problems or needs; (ii) learn to be patient, staying with initiatives long enough to make a difference; and (iii) identify intermediate goals and outcomes to help gauge how the initiative is coming along.

INTIMATE INVOLVEMENT OF KEY CONSTITUENCIES

Effective foundation programs are often characterized by true partnerships between the foundation and the other entities with which it is involved in attempting to address a social condition. A program that works involves entrepreneurial staffers who know how to listen, applicants with ideas to pursue, other independent perspectives and voices, time to nurture mutual understanding and respect, and an environment that fosters true partnerships.

The Balance of Power Conundrum: A major weakness of traditional philanthropy is perceived to be the power imbalance inherent in a relationship in which one party has money that the other party needs. It is perhaps the quintessential definition of the pragmatist's golden rule – "Those who have the gold rule!" – making true partnerships between grantors and grantees illusory.

This power relationship may have been more understandable when philanthropy consisted of a few wealthy individuals granting money to solve what they perceived to be the problems of others. And, many of today's largest and most influential foundations evolved directly from this model. However, with the extraordinary growth of new foundations, most of which are community-based, focused on local issues, and in close proximity to those with whom they work, accountability is much more immediate and tangible. As a result, foundations are placing increased emphasis on building relationships characterized by trust and equity with groups of people with whom they want to work, organizations whose capacities they want to harness, and institutions and systems they want to engage. This re-balancing of the power relationship between foundations and their grantees is one of the most significant challenges facing the field of philanthropy.

Involvement of Key Constituencies: Foundations increasingly perceive that engaging key constituents in every aspect of an initiative – from early conceptualization, through the establishment of goals, priorities, and strategy development, to implementation and assessment – significantly increases the likelihood that the initiative will be designed and implemented in such a way as to be successful. Accordingly, a critical first step in the development of a foundation program is to define those key constituencies that the program is designed to serve. Once key constituents are identified, they may be actively involved in creating the knowledge and understanding on which the program's design will be based, defining goals and priorities, formulating success criteria, and developing implementation strategies. Developing partnerships with key constituents also builds an audience for the program's ultimate results and products.

The Importance of External Inputs: There is a tendency among foundations to become isolated and parochial, gradually coming to believe that, as a function of their positions and viewpoints, they really *do* know what is best for the communities they serve. This is partly a result of the power imbalance discussed above, in which those in need of money find it difficult to tell foundation officers what they really think about their ideas, and partly a defensive reaction to the pressure of constantly being asked for money. It is imperative that foundations take every step possible to avoid this kind of thinking and the isolation it breeds.

Effective foundation programs emerge from, and flourish within, an environment in which intimate interactions with the brightest and most creative practitioners in a field of endeavor are both actively sought and highly valued. The contributions of these interactions can be sustained through the regular turnover of advisors, gaining the perspectives of "new blood" while, at the same time, avoiding the creation of an in-group that becomes stagnant.

MOBILIZING COMMUNITIES TO ADDRESS THEIR OWN PROBLEMS

Community Resources: Effective foundation programs recognize and engage the capacities within communities to solve their own problems. A corollary to the imbalance of power inherent in the relationship between foundations and those with whom they partner is the assumption underlying many foundation (and government) programs that communities lack the resources to solve their own problems. That assumption has led to a kind of co-dependency in which communities become dependent upon external forces and resources to solve their problems, and those external forces come to measure their effectiveness by how much they help communities.

This situation has important ramifications for all involved. Their dependence upon external forces for leadership and resources keeps communities fragmented and powerless, and inhibits the emergence of the indigenous leadership and capacities needed to solve today's problems and to prepare to solve tomorrow's. The delusion that external forces can, *in the long term,* solve the problems of communities leads foundations to overlook the latent resources within communities and to become frustrated and impatient as their programs fail to produce enduring improvement in social conditions. Moreover, as governments reduce the level of their commitment to solving social problems, foundations are increasingly being called upon to fill the resulting shortfall of resources. Since foundations don't come close to having the resources to make up these shortfalls, finding other approaches to addressing the social ills of communities is a growing imperative.

Solving Problems From the Inside Out: The approach gaining the most currency is using foundation resources to develop and build on the capacity of communities to identify and solve their own problems. This approach – solving community problems from the inside out – is based on the belief that many communities have the capacity to come together to address problems they perceive to be of high priority. If empowered to do so, communities can often organize themselves strategically to take on major problems.

For foundations, embracing this belief means catalyzing, facilitating, and supporting efforts by communities to pull together to: (i) define their own needs and priorities; (ii) establish the goals they wish to achieve and the time frame in which they hope to achieve them; (iii) figure out how to work together in such a way as to make a real difference in the quality of life of the community in which they live; and (iv) decide what kind of help they need from the outside.

This requires a whole new way of thinking on the part of foundations. Instead of defining what they think represent the most important problems facing communities, then trying to get local organizations to adapt their agendas to address those problems, foundations operating under this alternative paradigm see their role as helping communities think more strategically about the future, and mobilizing community resources in such a way that they not only contribute to the solution of specific problems of today, but can then be used to address the problems of tomorrow.

INFRASTRUCTURE DEVELOPMENT

An integral element of programmatic strategies aimed at mobilizing communities to address their own problems is helping communities build the infrastructure they require for sustained and effective action. Investing resources in such capacity-building reflects the recognition that: (i) effective community action results from the organized efforts of individuals and institutions within the community to bring about change; and (ii) helping those individuals and institutions realize their potential is a funding strategy with significant and enduring long-term payoffs.

Investing in Individuals: Ultimately, it is individuals who provide the leadership, commitment, and energy required for social change. While organizations often are the direct change agents, it is the individuals who create and lead those organizations who are responsible for establishing the environment in which change is possible. Foundations learn early on that a key to getting something done is getting the right person to do it – a person with a burning desire, the right experience and background, the capacity to bridge various worlds, and the ability to mobilize others.

Most creative foundation work comes from supporting such individuals – or teams of such individuals. There are huge differences among individuals and organizations in terms of these factors, and those who have them at one point in time may not be able to sustain them. Accordingly, skillful foundation officers soon learn how to: (i) identify such individuals and groups; (ii) provide the resources they need to make the best use of their creativity and talent; (iii) help them remain vital and effective; and (iv) help them move on when the time is right. They also learn to identify individuals and groups with the *potential* to be particularly creative and productive, and to provide the resources they need to fulfill that potential.

Given the important role of highly effective individuals in creating social improvement, development of tomorrow's leaders is a critical component of efforts to solve problems through community mobilization. Accordingly, a growing number of foundations are including leadership development activities in their programmatic strategies aimed at community improvement. An important element of such activities is interaction among the developing leaders aimed at the creation of enduring relationships and networks that, in the long term, will become a community's leadership infrastructure. This is consistent with the belief that investing in people has long-term ripple effects. Individuals touched by leadership development programs not only go on to do great things themselves, but they influence those with whom they come in contact, diffusing a sense of possibility and potential throughout their community.

Investing in Institutions: While individuals play a key role in mobilizing the talent, energy, and resources required for change, it is organizations that implement the service, advocacy, knowledge development, education, and policy programs through which foundations achieve the goals of their programs. Accordingly, an important element of foundation efforts to build the problem-solving capacities of communities is developing, nurturing, and sustaining the organizations whose ongoing activities directly affect the lives of individuals and families. This may involve providing support for technical assistance, the filling of key staff positions, fund-raising consultants, and core operations – anything it takes to sustain and strengthen organizations whose activities fill vital community needs.

There is tendency among foundations to eschew general operating support for organizations providing social services. They would much rather fund the establishment of new organizational entities or the development of innovative new programs than support an organization's ongoing operations. Unfortunately, with governments cutting back their support for social service and safety net programs, these organizations have few places to turn for resources to sustain their bread-and-butter activities and support their underlying infrastructure. Accordingly, foundation's are faced with the challenge of helping to sustain organizations that play a central role in a foundation's program strategies while at the same time supporting the development and testing of new and innovative approaches to addressing social problems and needs.

THE ROLE OF COMMUNICATIONS

Communications are increasingly being perceived to be powerful allies in helping foundations attain their programmatic goals. Rather than constituting a footnote or afterthought to a program, as has traditionally been the case, communication strategies are envisioned as integral elements of every program undertaken by foundations. Such strategies include: (i) communicating the goals and expectations of the program to diverse audiences; (ii) helping build a constituency for the program's results and outcomes; (iii) providing practical information to people on the results of programs and their implications for individuals, families, and communities, and how they can be applied in practice; (iv) drawing attention to the role of the foundation in a particular field and to the work of its grantees; and (v) disseminating program results to others working on similar problems.

Foundations active in the realm of public policy employ aggressive communication strategies as integral elements of their efforts to raise public awareness and educate public officials about a particular issue. In a complicated world in which most public policy issues are polarized and contentious, these foundations view their role as serving as credible, neutral sources of information that can help people understand all sides of an issue, as well as building a consensus for a particular approach to addressing social issues and problems.

No matter the purpose, effective use of communications requires paying attention to constituents, carefully matching the strategy employed to the target audience and desired impact. It is important to be clear, from the beginning, on what the foundation is trying to achieve, whom it is trying to reach, and at what scale it will be working, and to select a communications strategy that is consistent with these specifications.

Chapter 5: Self-Assessment: Measuring, Learning, Improving

THE EVALUATION CONUNDRUM

How to demonstrate the effectiveness of individual programs and their collective impacts is one of the greatest challenges facing foundation boards and staffs. As a result, evaluation is an ongoing focus of attention for virtually every foundation. Foundation Boards and staffs are asking questions such as:

- To whom are we accountable? To what degree does that accountability require us to demonstrate the overall value of what we do?

- To what degree is it even possible for us to demonstrate the overall value of what we do? If it is possible, how can we do it most convincingly?

- Does a commitment to evaluation mean that we can only pursue programs for which there are measurable outcomes? If not, how do we go about assessing the impacts of programs dealing with larger social conditions, where change takes a long time, large secular processes are at work, and the foundation is but a bit player?

- Is evaluation primarily a tool for helping us make funding decisions (summative evaluation) or for helping us and our grantees learn how to improve what we do (formative evaluation)?

- Should we evaluate all funded projects, no matter their scope and cost? How much should we spend on evaluation?

- What is the right mix between quantitative and qualitative evaluation methods?

- What structures, processes, and incentives do we need to put in place to create an environment in which learning is encouraged, facilitated, and rewarded?

WHY IS IT SO HARD?

The Nature of the Beast: That questions such as these should prove so vexing to virtually all foundations is a reflection of the nature of the foundation beast, its raison d'etre, and how it operates. Because foundations are free from the usual accountability imposed by voters, stockholders, or contributors, there are no commonly accepted standards against which to measure the effectiveness and impact of what they do. This lack of benchmarks and performance criteria is exacerbated by the fact that many foundations believe their mission to be changing social conditions and institutions in such a way as to bring about major improvements in people's lives – outcomes that are neither easily quantifiable or measurable nor readily traceable to a foundation's interventions.

So, To Whom *Are* We Answerable? To a large degree, foundations are accountable to themselves. Yes, they are required to adhere to certain federal and state laws and regulations concerning how they manage their assets, how much of their assets they must distribute each year, and, in general terms, the kinds of activities and organizations they can and cannot fund. However, within these broad guidelines, they are largely free to use the resources at their disposal in any way they deem consistent with their mission. They have extremely broad discretion and, depending on the thickness of their skins, can do pretty much as they see fit.

That said, foundations – the boards of which are comprised largely of accomplished, well-connected, and visible business, financial, legal, academic, and community leaders – are sensitive to what they perceive to be their obligation to use their resources to advance the public good. Obligation to whom, then, becomes an important question. And, in the end, it comes down to a combination of:

The Donor – The source of the resources that make up the foundation's asset base. Even in those cases where little direction was provided by the donor, foundation boards generally endeavor to fashion programs that are consistent with the donor's intent.

Society at Large – The broad society in which the foundation exists (particularly in the case of the larger national foundations) or the immediate community in which the foundation is located and operates (the case for community foundations and most of the new "conversion" foundations).

This means that the over-arching question the foundation feels obligated to address is: Are we making the world a better place?

The Foundation Itself – The board comes to recognize that, ultimately, it is answerable to itself in the form of its board of trustees or directors.

The Nature of Accountability: Rather than being a source of comfort, the fact that a foundation is essentially answerable to itself turns out to be a source of considerable angst and trepidation among members of foundation boards. And in some cases, it may actually compel a foundation board to be more conservative and more concerned with demonstrating success and avoiding failure than it would be if the foundation were accountable to specific external authorities.

This is part of the evaluation conundrum: Depending on how it is perceived and carried out, accountability can be either a motivator or restraint. As a motivator, accountability can serve as a force for clarity of purpose, strategic action, appropriate assessment, and, in the end, greater accomplishment. As a restraint, accountability can hobble bold action, the pursuit of unpopular causes, and the tackling of major challenges against which progress may be difficult to document. In order to be able to make a difference in the social realms in which they work, foundations have to be willing to take risks, to understand up front that failure is a possibility, and to view failure not as something to be avoided at all costs – lest it be the target of external criticism – but as an opportunity to learn. *Given the tremendous needs that exist, the greatest failure for a foundation is to be so paralyzed by the fear of failure and the preoccupation with quantitative outcomes, that it ends up doing nothing significant at all.*

THE CASE FOR SELF-ASSESSMENT

Self-assessment – the process through which foundations examine the overall value of their philanthropic activities – represents the next frontier in organized philanthropy. Given their important oversight responsibilities, foundation boards are keenly interested in knowing how their foundations are doing in terms of fulfilling their missions and meeting their goals. Yet in the end, the "so what?" question almost always goes unanswered. In part, this is due to the exigencies of the processes through which grants are approved and awarded; in part, it is due to the difficulty of trying to meet the many challenges and exploit the many opportunities facing philanthropy. They just simply never get to it! However, by far the greatest barrier to self-assessment is the difficulty inherent in trying to define and measure the relative contributions of foundation programs to changes in the lives of individuals, families, and communities. This challenge often proves sufficiently formidable that it is relegated to tomorrow's agenda.

The Key Question: What Have We Accomplished? To begin the process of self-assessment, foundations need to reach the point where they are ready to address the most important questions they face as organizations: What have we accomplished with the resources we've deployed to date? Not what has each of our individual projects achieved; not even what has each of our major programs achieved. But, what does it all add up to? What difference have we made as a foundation? Can we justify our existence? Can we make a compelling case for why we should continue to enjoy our considerable tax advantages? While most foundations may wish to avoid these questions, they represent the core challenge to the field of philanthropy.

Weaving Self-Assessment Into a Foundation's Fabric: It is characteristic of most foundations that the preponderance of staff time and energy is devoted to the demands of the pre-grant process (triaging and reviewing proposals, performing due-diligence on potential grantees, preparing recommendations for the board, and awarding grants). This leaves relatively little for such post-award processes as facilitating the work of grantees, pulling together the various elements of complex programs or initiatives, monitoring grantee progress, reading grantee reports and evaluations, and learning about what has worked and what hasn't. And even less attention is paid by board and staff to reflecting on what the foundation's programs add up to and what difference they are making overall.

Increasingly, foundations are coming to believe that as part of their accountability to themselves, as well as to the society around them, they need to make self-assessment a much more integral and self-conscious part of everything they do. Accordingly, they are taking steps to create the time, space, and organizational structures required to increase both the salience and priority of self-reflection and learning. This includes:

Setting Aside Formal Opportunities for Self-Examination – Making learning and self-assessment institutional priorities, and creating regular, formal opportunities for boards and staffs to reflect on what they are doing, determine what is working and what isn't, and consider how best to apply lessons learned to improving programs and increasing their impacts;

Collecting Information From External Sources – Using a variety of mechanisms, including formal evaluations, qualitative assessments, site visits, commissioned studies, and surveys of grantees, applicants, and various constituencies, to obtain a wide range of external perspectives on what the foundation is doing and how well it is doing it;

Extracting and Applying Lessons Learned – Analyzing information obtained from these various sources, extracting the most valuable lessons about how the foundation can maximize its effectiveness and impacts, and applying those lessons, in a rigorous way, to improving its policies, programs, and processes. Too often, the reams of data foundations collect about their programs languish on the shelves of staff offices for lack of structured processes for using the information; and

Disseminating Lessons learned – Making a strong commitment to overcoming the myopia and isolation that characterize many foundations, sharing with other foundations and with various constituencies what has been learned from formal evaluations, grantee reports, and a foundation's own reflections on what has worked and what hasn't.

GUIDING PRINCIPLES

A number of principles are emerging from the experiences of foundations grappling with the "so what?" question.

An Effective Institutional Culture is One that Values Learning:

Foundations committed to self-assessment as a vehicle for constantly increasing the impact of what they do create institutional environments that foster and reward learning. In those environments: (i) grant making is viewed as a mechanism for learning about what works and what doesn't; (ii) attempting to change social systems and address underlying causes of social ills is understood to be antithetical to neat, clean solutions and outcomes; (iii) board and staff question what it means in the business of philanthropy to make mistakes; (iv) the process of trying, testing, learning, and applying lessons learned is valued as a viable modus operandi; and (v) no one has to be defensive when things don't work out as planned.

Evaluation is Principally a Tool for Learning: Foundations that adopt learning as an institutional priority change their perceptions about the role of evaluation and evaluators. They come to view evaluation less as a source of data on which to make summary judgments about grants and programs, than as an ongoing source of information about program strengths that can be exploited and program weaknesses that can be remedied, as the foundation continually improves the quality and impacts of what it does.

Effective Learning is Dependent on the Clarity of Expected Outcomes: The ability of a foundation to learn from its assessments of individual grants, of complex program initiatives, and of its overall effectiveness as an organization, depends in large part on the degree to which it has articulated, up front, clear goals, objectives, and expected outcomes. Lack of clarity on what a foundation is trying to accomplish makes it almost impossible to determine whether it is accomplishing it.

Goals Should Serve as Motivators Not Shackles: Foundation boards and staffs should set program goals, objectives, and expected outcomes high enough that they serve as ambitious targets toward which they are constantly striving, rather than setting them at a level determined by what is measurable.

Assessment is Cradle to Grave: The most effective assessment strategies are those that are integral elements of a grant or program, from initial conceptualization to completion. This concurrent approach to learning is based on a continuous feedback model of assessment in which information obtained is applied to improving the project or program on an ongoing basis.

Effective Assessment is a Partnership: Assessments that work best and achieve the most are those in which the foundation and its partners engage in a process of mutual learning, rather than a process which is imposed by the foundation.

Effective Assessment Strategies Produce Information Measured by its Usefulness Rather Than by its Volume: In their zeal to evaluate what they are doing, foundations often fall into the trap of depending on quantitative evaluation technologies to produce hard data on soft outcomes that do not lend themselves to rigorous analysis. In such cases, the reams of data produced may actually serve to obscure reality and constrain appropriate action by the foundation. A more effective approach involves a mix of quantitative measures of outcomes, when appropriate, and direct observation of the situation in which the foundation is working.

Effective Self-Assessment Requires an Effective Board: The foundation board plays a crucial role in establishing self-assessment as a priority, in creating an environment in which self-assessment is valued and practiced, and in applying the results of self-assessment to improving the foundation's performance. To play such a role most effectively, boards should: (i) comprise individuals who are knowledgeable and experienced in areas related to those in which the foundation works; (ii) bring to the table a breadth and diversity of perspectives on the world in which the foundation operates; (iii) have independent sources of information to balance that brought by the staff; and (iv) insist that everything undertaken by the foundation has clear purposes, goals, expected outcomes, and criteria for success, agreed upon in advance.

III.
Organizing for Maximum Impact

Introduction

Having discussed the challenges facing philanthropy, and the approaches foundations might employ to meet those challenges in the most effective way, let's look more closely at foundations as organizations. Interestingly, with all the things written about the institution of philanthropy, precious little of that literature addresses these unusual entities in terms of their organizational structure and function and how they might be optimized to maximize effectiveness and impact. Just as it is assumed that anyone can do grantmaking (giving away money is easy, isn't it?), it is assumed that any organizational structure will do for a foundation. The following four chapters give the lie to that notion, explaining how responsible governance, excellent leadership, professional staff, and thoughtful organizational design contribute individually and collectively to making foundations effective institutions. An important lesson to be drawn from this section is how important it is to look at the entirety of a foundation systematically, understanding the critical roles of each organizational element, how each relates to others, and how they add up to an organization that is more than the sum of its individual units and functions.

Chapter 6: The Board is Where it All Starts

INTRODUCTION

Effective philanthropy starts with effective governance. It is the members of the governing board who have the ultimate authority and accountability for management and disposition of a foundation's assets, for setting the organization's directions and policies, and for assuring that they are implemented in such a way as to maximize progress toward achievement of the foundation's mission and goals. Yet, relatively little attention is paid to the role of the board in philanthropy. Philanthropy is not like other societal enterprises, and foundations are not like other organizations. For both to succeed, their distinctive features have to be recognized and taken into account by governing boards, then translated into appropriate governing principles, processes, and styles.

This is not to say that philanthropy cannot benefit a great deal from borrowing some of the practices that have been effective in business, academia, and other eleemosynary organizations. However, their wholesale transfer to this distinctive setting seldom leads to salutary outcomes. Examples include: (i) the imposition on grantees of strict financial accountability measures, as a surrogate for what we really care about, i.e., program impacts; (ii) attempts to establish quantitative outcomes and milestones for foundation programs, in spite of the woeful state of our ability to measure social change, and to attribute any change detected to a foundation's efforts; (iii) the use of financial incentives to motivate program staff, despite the lack of appropriate measures of the effectiveness of staff as grantmakers; and (iv) more recently, the application to philanthropy of the strategies of venture capital, despite the huge differences in the two enterprises, and the lack of evidence that such strategies add value to the relationship between foundations and their grantees.

Like effective philanthropy, effective foundation governance doesn't just happen. Since foundation boards* are involved on a part-time basis, meeting only a few times a year, exploiting the opportunities open to them and ful-

* While foundation board members are, in some cases, directors, and in others, trustees, in this volume, they are referred to as directors.

filling the obligations they have assumed are particularly difficult challenges. Yet, they must meet those challenges, for the stakes are too high to do anything less. At a minimum, members of foundation boards must debunk the myth that the board room doorway contains a device that blurs the judgment of directors as they enter and erases their memories as they leave!

BOARD ROLES AND RESPONSIBILITIES

Foundation governing boards are stewards of a public trust whose financial resources are protected from taxation as long as they are managed prudently, and expended to benefit the public good, and whose independent status is honored as long as it is managed with integrity and wisdom. Essentially, a foundation board has five principal obligations.

Asset Management: Foundations, even small ones, are significant corporate entities with substantial financial resources. The protection, management, and expenditure of those resources are the board's principal legal and moral obligations. This fiduciary responsibility includes:

Prudent Investment – Protecting and managing the foundation's financial assets responsibly and prudently so that they produce the growth and return necessary to meet or exceed distribution requirements over the long term. The board of a foundation serves as trustees of its assets. As such, they have a duty to make prudent investment decisions in the acquisition or sale of any assets. This duty includes, but is not limited to: (i) development of asset management policies consistent with the foundation's long-term goals and payout requirements; (ii) diligence and vigilance in overseeing the implementation of those policies and assessing their effectiveness and appropriateness; (iii) diversification within the investment portfolio; (iv) avoidance of speculative investments, waste, unnecessary taxes, and penalties; and (v) compliance with state and federal requirements.

Wise Expenditure – Allocating a foundation's financial assets as effectively as possible to advance its mission and attain its goals, so that: (i) grantmaking programs and other mission-related activities are on target, knowledge-based, well-designed, and professionally implemented; (ii) administrative and capital expenditures are prudent, reasonable, and consistent with the organization's status as a non-profit, eleemosynary entity; and (iii) annual plans and budgets are carefully developed, based on sound reasoning and financial principles, and faithfully adhered to.

Careful Accounting and Reporting – Assuring that the organization has in place the systems needed for careful monitoring of expenditures, highly professional accounting and record-keeping, regular external audits, and assiduous adherence to all reporting requirements.

Involvement of Every Board Member – Making sure that every member of a foundation board shares in the responsibility for protecting and managing the foundation's assets and overseeing their expenditure. While directors can delegate certain functions to committees or staff, and can rely on outside experts for advice and counsel, *they can neither delegate their ultimate fiduciary obligations, nor depend on others to fulfill them.* Recent scandals at nonprofit organizations, including foundations, demonstrate what can happen when board members are asleep at the fiduciary wheel.

Establishment of Directions, Priorities, and Policies: The board creates the operational framework that governs everything a foundation does: (i) articulating the direction in which the foundation heads; (ii) setting the priorities it pursues; (iii) establishing the policies under which it operates; and (iv) defining the boundaries within which the CEO and staff can act.

Oversight of Staff Implementation: With the operational framework in place, the board monitors and oversees its implementation by the organization's chief staff officer. This includes the hiring and firing of that officer; regular assessments of his or her performance; measurement of progress in meeting financial, programmatic, and operational goals; and remedial actions intended to improve the organization's overall effectiveness and efficiency.

Keeping the Foundation's Eye on the Prize: The board is the keeper of the foundation's mission, constantly reminding itself, the staff, and others why the foundation exists, and flying the banner behind which everyone is expected to march. In fulfilling this responsibility, directors represent a tremendous asset to the foundation, serving as critical links between the foundation and the communities and constituencies it exists to serve, as eyes and ears on the outside world, and as ambassadors to that outside world.

Being Accountable: Perhaps the most daunting of a foundation board's obligations is its accountability for expending the foundation's limited resources in such a way as to have maximum impact on the problems it chooses to address. The independence that frees a foundation from externally imposed constraints imposes on the board the responsibility for:

(i) establishing clear goals, expectations, and priorities; (ii) deciding how best to deploy resources to meet them; (iii) creating criteria and measures of performance; (iv) implementing appropriate assessment strategies; and (v) applying the lessons learned from those assessments to improving overall performance, impact, and outcomes. While the board may employ outside experts to evaluate the foundation's performance, and may value the views of others concerning its success, in the end, directors are answerable to themselves. Depending on how you look at it, this can be a blessing or a curse!

PRINCIPLES OF GOOD GOVERNANCE

Taken as a whole, these roles and responsibilities constitute a significant challenge for any foundation director. Fulfilling them in a way that maximizes the effectiveness of the foundation's governance, programs, and operations means that foundation board members must:

- Come to grips with the full ramifications of what it means to exercise fiduciary responsibility for a public trust;

- Consider the implications and consequences of today's decisions for the foundation's long-term integrity, effectiveness, and impact;

- Balance personal beliefs and agendas with the foundation's long-term mission, and with their responsibility for protecting the integrity of the foundation's governance and operational processes;

- Remember that they are members of a board that, as a group, is responsible for advancing the foundation's mission and meeting its goals. While they bring to the board their distinctive perspectives of particular population groups, they do not represent those groups as though they were their constituents;

- Operate in a trusting, cohesive, and collegial manner, able to resolve contentious issues and concerns as a team, and to speak to the outside world with a single voice;

- "Steer not row," assiduously avoiding the temptation to get involved in program implementation and operations management, and respecting the roles, responsibilities, and prerogatives of the staff;

- Adhere to a policy of strict confidentiality concerning all board discussions, actions, decisions, and materials; and

- Recognize and deal with actual, potential, or apparent conflicts of interest promptly and openly.

CONDUCT AND BEHAVIOR

Along with a foundation's programmatic reach and prominence come opportunities for conflicts between the responsibilities of board members to the foundation and their interest in, and loyalties to, other organizations and individuals. Accordingly, it is important that boards adopt standards of conduct and behavior designed to: (i) protect the integrity of their decision-making and governance processes; (ii) preserve the quality, fairness, and openness of foundation program development, review, funding, and oversight mechanisms; and (iii) shield board members from inappropriate intrusions on their time, privacy, and other personal and professional interests and responsibilities.

A foundation's ability to engage the partners with which it must work to achieve its goals depends on the degree to which its policies, practices, and procedures are characterized by fairness and equity. It is the responsibility of the staff to assure that this fundamental principle is translated into practice through the development and consistent application of grant making policies and procedures. It is the responsibility of the board to assure that this fundamental principle is adhered to, by: (i) being familiar with the policies and procedures established by the staff, and supporting their conscientious and rigorous implementation; (ii) maintaining the "thick line" between the board and the staff, communicating issues and concerns with, or through, the chief staff officer; (iii) maintaining the even "thicker line" between the foundation and the organizations with which it does business, communicating issues and concerns with, or through, the chief staff officer; and (iv) minimizing conflicts between their other personal and professional activities and affiliations and their responsibilities and obligations to the foundation.

Practices: Fulfilling the board's guidance and oversight functions requires that each director jealously protect board objectivity and impartiality by maintaining an arms-length distance from the design of specific initiatives, the preparation and submission of specific proposals, the review of proposals, and the review and oversight of funded projects, and from foundation-related activities of prospective or actual foundation grantees. The following practices are designed to help foundation directors protect their standing as objective and impartial judges of the foundation's destination and the best route to that destination, and to shield them from organizations and individuals wishing to exploit their relationships or access for the purpose of gaining an advantage in obtaining or maintaining foundation funding.

Avoid Commenting: Directors should do what they can to avoid situations in which they are asked to: (i) comment on ideas, concepts, or projects, in terms of their merit or appropriateness; (ii) review written letters of intent or proposals being considered for submission to the foundation for funding; or (iii) respond to complaints about foundation funding decisions or staff handling of letters of interest, proposals, or ongoing grants. Acceding to such requests almost always backfires, putting board members in extremely awkward situations vis-à-vis other directors, staff members, and outside organizations.

Deny Influence on Review Processes: When approached, board members should stress: (i) the impossibility and inappropriateness of board involvement in individual proposals and projects; (ii) the board's role in providing overall direction and oversight of foundation programs, rather than in designing, reviewing, or overseeing individual projects; and (iii) the reliance of the board on a professional staff charged with implementing impartial, fair, and objective processes for program development, proposal review, and grant oversight.

Refer to Published Guidelines: Directors can, in the long run, be more helpful by: (i) assisting prospective grantees in obtaining copies of the foundation's published program guidelines; (ii) putting the onus on the organization to determine the degree of fit between the proposed work and the foundation's interests and requirements; (iii) stressing the importance of adhering to the processes through which the foundation identifies projects it wishes to pursue; and (iv) pointing out that attempting to short-circuit this process serves only to delay, and perhaps jeopardize, the foundation's consideration of ideas that may be worthy.

Conflicts of Interest: Members of a foundation's board are capable, prominent, and active individuals with multiple areas of personal and professional interest and involvement. It is *inevitable* that situations will arise in which the board must reach a decision about an organization or activity in which one of its members has an interest that represents an actual or apparent conflict. There are three critical elements to policies designed to minimize the consequences of such conflicts of interest – awareness, disclosure, and disinterested review:

Awareness – It is the responsibility of each director to be vigilant and sensitive about situations that represent actual or apparent conflicts between his or her obligation to the foundation and an interest in another organization or activity.

Disclosure – Whenever a conflict of interest is identified, it should be disclosed well in advance of any board or committee discussion or action in which the conflict is a factor.

Disinterested Review – It is the responsibility of the board to assure that its decisions are based on objective reviews and analyses.

It is imperative that, as early in its existence as possible, every foundation adopt a conflict of interest policy based on these principles (see Appendix A for a model policy). To reinforce the importance of this policy and the objectivity and fairness of board decision making it is intended to protect, it is recommended that board members:

• Adhere to the practices discussed above with respect to involvement with organizations seeking foundation funding;

• Be highly sensitive to those situations in which there is any actual or apparent conflict between one's responsibility to the foundation and involvement in another organization;

• Disclose any and all such real or apparent conflicts, in writing, via the annual disclosure form (see Appendix A for model disclosure form), supplemented by letters to the board chair and the chief staff officer, when appropriate; and

• Identify such conflicts prior to any consideration, discussion, or decision by the full board or board committee and *absent themselves from the room during deliberations directly related to decisions and votes.* While the board may wish to obtain the views of the conflicted director concerning the organization in which he or she is involved, once that information is imparted, the involved member should recuse himself or herself until a decision has been reached. *It is unacceptable for a board member to observe the votes of his or her colleagues on a transaction in which he or she has a conflict.*

Board Protocol: Maximizing the value of governance requires that a foundation board operate in a manner that is consistent with certain behavioral norms.

Attendance – It is expected that, when an individual agrees to serve on a foundation board, he or she accepts the responsibility of participating in all board meetings, and in all meetings of the committees on which he or she serves. While it is understood that circumstances will arise that preclude board members from attending meetings, it is expected that this will be a rare exception, with foundation meetings accorded high priority when conflicts arise.

Preparation for Meetings – The smooth and efficient operation of a board depends on directors arriving at meetings fully prepared for the discussions to be held, decisions to be made, and actions to be taken. Board materials should be sent out well in advance of each meeting to allow ample time for members to review them – and to raise questions or concerns with the chief staff officer – prior to their arrival at the meeting.

Maintenance of Open Communications – The effectiveness of each director, as well as of the board as a whole, depends upon open communication among members, and between the board and the staff, primarily via the chief staff officer. As stated earlier in this section, fulfilling their considerable obligations and responsibilities requires that directors interact in a way that is respectful of each other's opinions and perspectives, and work as a group to make policies, decisions, and actions that are, in all cases, in the best interest of the foundation.

Board-Staff Relations – While the board bears ultimate responsibility for the management and expenditure of the foundation's assets, it is the staff that has the responsibility for its day-to-day financial transactions, administration, and operations, and grant making programs. It is critical that there be developed and sustained a relationship between the board and the staff characterized by mutual trust, respect, and collegiality, and an organizational climate in which staff are respected and their work for the foundation valued.

BUILDING AN EFFECTIVE BOARD

Effective governing boards don't just happen! They are carefully and assiduously designed, built, nurtured, and supported. While that assertion holds true for all organizations, it needs to be firmly imprinted in the minds of everyone involved in the operation of a foundation. All foundation board members, staff members, and outside constituents should understand that the success of the foundation they serve, or are served by, depends on the quality of its governance. In this case, quality implies:

- A solid vision and understanding of the board's roles and responsibilities, and what it takes to fulfill them;

- Involvement of individuals representing the perspectives, expertise, and experience the board needs to fulfill its governance obligations assisted by regular turnover in board membership;

- Commitment to philanthropy as a means of improving the human condition, and to the foundation as an instrument for pursuing that vision;

- Single-minded pursuit of the foundation's mission and goals;

- Strong fiduciary, programmatic, and operational direction and oversight;

- A major focus on ongoing learning as a means of knowing as much as possible about the environment in which the foundation operates, emerging issues, progress toward achievement of the foundation's goals, and the performance of the board itself;

- Input from a variety of internal and external sources; and

- Strong, responsive, support systems and structures, and operating styles.

Developing a Long-Term Vision: The founding boards of new foundations are preoccupied with creating organizations from scratch, establishing the initial program focuses, strategies, and operating styles, reviewing the quality of early grants, recruiting the first chief staff officer, and assuring the appropriateness and effectiveness of organizational management and administration – all under the constant pressure to make payout. And, once foundations are established, their boards become fully occupied with carrying out their significant governance roles, letting slide the kind of self-reflection and planning they need to remain effective as the organization grows and matures. As a result, foundation boards generally evolve in response to problems as they emerge, rather than by proactively addressing their roles, operational styles, and composition.

At some point, however, it is incumbent upon members of foundation boards

to take a hard look at themselves, establishing a regular process for thoughtful and deliberate reflection on how they have operated to date, what they
have learned from that experience, and where there is room for improvement.
This self-reflection establishes the basis on which to formulate a plan for
building on their strengths and correcting their weaknesses. The first step in
that process is articulation of a vision of the board's obligations, responsibilities, and capabilities. With that vision in mind, the board can manage its
capabilities in ways that are consistent with maximizing its long-term effectiveness as a governing body, and establish the best working relationships.

Board Composition: Building and sustaining a board with the diversity,
professional competence, and mission it needs for high quality governance
requires an intensive, focused effort involving all directors. This implies a systematic approach to developing a board comprising just the right mix of people needed to fulfill its full range of roles and responsibilities. Such an
approach should include: (i) analysis of the implications of the board's long-
term vision for board composition in terms of diversity of perspectives, expertise, and experience; (ii) formulation of a list of what the board needs to carry
out its roles most effectively; (iii) establishment of criteria for use in the selection of new members; and (iv) an intensive process of candidate identification, vetting, and recruitment.

Criteria for Recruitment and Retention: Foundation board members
should be elected or re-elected on the basis of criteria that reflect the board's
vision of its obligations and roles, and what it needs to fulfill them, rather than
on cronyism, favoritism, or elitism. In general, members of a foundation board
should be selected or retained on the basis of:

• What They Know – Solid competence and experience in one or more critical areas of board function, such as organizational leadership, program
  direction and oversight, asset management, finance, knowledge of the communities in which the foundation works and of the people the foundation
  serves, and the workings of the nonprofit sector;

• Who They Are – Their stature in their communities; the breadth of their
  contacts and interactions in those communities; and the perspectives they
  bring to the board from their racial, ethnic, and cultural backgrounds,
  training, personal experiences, and professional lives;

• How They Interact with Others – Their ability to work well as members of a governance team, treat other board members with respect, and sublimate their own biases, interests, and passions when it is in the best interest of the foundation to do so; and

- Their Level of Commitment – A strong commitment to the foundation's vision, mission, and grantmaking programs; the willingness and ability to devote the time and energy required to meet their responsibilities as board members; and the capacity to act first and foremost as sound stewards of the foundation and its resources.

Diversity: Increasingly, the people served by foundations represent a diversity of racial, ethnic, and cultural backgrounds. This reality has huge implications for all foundations – no matter the origin of their assets, their size, their substantive focus, or their location or geographic purview – and for the design and implementation of all their programs. And, since to be able to govern most effectively, foundation boards must reflect the diversity of the people their foundations exist to serve, this reality has implications, too, for the composition of the board and staff.

In the end, a foundation board should be comprised of individuals who bring to its deliberations: (i) a richness of perspectives that assures that the foundation's eye is always on *The Prize* of improving the condition of *all* the people it exists to serve; (ii) an independence of thinking that assures that basic assumptions are challenged, alternative points of view are introduced, and questions from outside the box are raised; and (iii) the ability to work as part of a governance team in which every member, opinion, and idea is accorded equal attention and respect.

Building and maintaining such a board requires vigilance and thoughtful planning throughout the foundation's existence. An important product of the systematic approach to board composition and operation described above should be the development of an overall sense of what the board ought to look like in order to carry out its obligations to its principal constituents. A major challenge is building and maintaining an appropriately diverse board without reserving "slots" for representatives of specific groups of people. Instead, boards should implement a process for searching far and wide for individuals who bring to the board the expertise and experiences it needs to do its business in the most effective way, making sure that, in meeting the criteria it has established for selecting members, the board reflects, to the degree possible and appropriate, the diversity of the people served by the programs it supports. If, the board's search process goes beyond the "usual suspects" to individuals of every racial, ethnic, and cultural group, and economic class, the foundation will end up with the diverse board it needs to carry out its governance functions most effectively.

An important but often overlooked aspect of diversity is social and economic class. There is a strong tendency among foundation boards to be attracted to highly educated, articulate, and socially adept individuals who represent a class of people used to, and comfortable with, serving on such boards. However, there are many people who, while from the opposite end of the class spectrum, are bright, capable, and able to hold their own on a foundation board. Because the usual nomination processes fail to identify such individuals, foundations must employ candidate search strategies capable of going beyond the "usual suspects." This is particularly important for those foundations whose programs primarily address the needs of the poor and underserved.

Another challenge is making sure that critical expertise, perspectives, or experiences reside in more than one person. When boards have only one person, or one dominant person, with a particular viewpoint, expertise, or background, there is the danger that such a person will come to be seen as the expert in, or the spokesperson for, a particular topic, issue, or group. Gradually, discussions, decisions, and actions become dominated by the views and biases of such individuals. For the board, the danger is that it will become too easy for members to defer to a particular colleague when considering an issue in his or her area of expertise or interest. For the individual, the danger is that he or she becomes the token spokesperson, coming to feel that he or she must speak up for that issue every time.

An effectively diverse board is one that, over time, becomes multi-cultural. On such a board, all members are concerned with all the people and issues the foundation exists to serve; directors represent perspectives, not single issues or groups of people; those perspectives reflect sensitivities to particular characteristics, cultures, and situations derived from the directors' distinctive backgrounds and experiences; and all issues are fair game for in-depth exploration.

MAINTAINING AN EFFECTIVE BOARD

Just as building an effective board requires care and diligence, so does its nurturing and maintenance. Keeping a board's collective eye on *The Prize*, sustaining its vitality and effectiveness, and keeping it in touch with reality represent significant challenges that must be met if the foundation governed by the board is to live up to its potential as an instrument of social improvement. The following represent some elements of a comprehensive strategy for keeping foundation boards productive and on target.

Regular Turnover: Turnover in the membership of a foundation board is essential to its continued relevance and effectiveness over the long term. While well-functioning boards constantly learn and grow, regular changes in composition help keep a board "fresh," preventing the staleness, comfort, and complacency that eventually threaten the creativity, productivity, and aptness of all governing bodies. No matter the substantive focus of a foundation's grantmaking, the programmatic strategies it employs, or the communities it serves, the environment in which it operates is constantly changing. Recent examples include: the huge economic swings of the last decade; the ongoing shifts in the makeup of the country's population; recent upheavals in the nation's systems of health care; advances in deciphering the human genome, in applying stem cells to reducing the suffering due to disorders such as spinal cord injury and Parkinson's Disease, and in understanding the long-term effects of global warming; and the extraordinarily rapid growth in the use of electronic communications such as the Internet and other wireless technologies.

While the need for regular turnover in membership is generally accepted in theory, the reduction of that theory to practice is often problematic, particularly when it applies to the founding board of a new foundation. For several reasons, board members of foundations are often reluctant to step aside. Serving on a foundation board represents an unparalleled opportunity for an individual to contribute to the solution of important social problems; it is prestigious and it may represent a source of income. But perhaps even more important, board members often come to identify themselves with the foundation, to feel that retaining their special understanding of the foundation and its origins and purposes outweighs the need for fresh perspectives, ideas, competencies, and experiences, and to value the relationships they have formed with other board members. These are all valid considerations. However, they reflect a failure to put the best interests of the foundation before the personal interests of its board members. In the long term, an institution whose ultimate purpose is improving social conditions must: (i) establish and enforce board terms and term limits; (ii) constantly be on the lookout for the kinds of new members it needs to remain relevant and effective; and (iii) put in place mechanisms for maintaining institutional memory and culture, and for orienting new members.

Orientation of New Members: A key element in the acculturation of new board members is systematic and effective orientation. The purpose of orientation is to bring new members up to speed as rapidly as possible about the foundation and its programs; to impart the knowledge and experience gained by current and past board members; and to sustain, to the degree possible and appropriate, the board's modus operandi, culture, and momentum. Most foundations devote little attention to orientation of new members, assuming that they will learn on the job. However, a formal and systematic orientation process will help minimize the disruption of the ongoing work of the board and accelerate the assimilation of new members. Such a process should include, at a minimum, information on:

- Philanthropy as a social institution;

- Foundations as instruments of that institution;

- The roles and responsibilities of foundation boards, in general;

- This board's vision of its purpose, modus operandi, composition, and operational style; and

- This foundation's history, mission, values, and priorities; grantmaking programs; organizational structure; and modus operandi.

Orientation is part of the board's ongoing process of learning, involving, at a minimum, sessions before board meetings, individual meetings with current and past members and key staff, and the maintenance of a comprehensive board manual containing important documents, policies, procedures, and program materials.

Board Structures, Processes, and Information: To be effective, governing boards must have in place the structures and processes they need to get their work done. As a rule, these evolve absent an overall plan, responding to needs and problems as they arise. As a result, many foundation boards lack the supports, mechanisms, and information they need to be maximally effective. Early in the development of new foundations, and regularly through the life of established ones, attention should be focused on defining, developing, and institutionalizing the policies, structures, and processes the board needs to support its governance roles and responsibilities. This process should be derivative of the one the board goes through to establish and reassess its vision, roles and responsibilities, its governance strategies, and its relationships with the chief staff officer, other staff members, and the outside world.

Board Committees: Committees represent a strategy for delegating to a smaller number of directors, responsibility for oversight of specific aspects of the organization's functioning. When implemented appropriately, this strategy can make a major contribution to a board's capacity to carry out its numerous functions efficiently. When abused, the strategy leads to diffusion of authority and responsibility, fewer people with knowledge of all aspects of a foundation's programs and operations, and inappropriate intrusion into the operational domain of the staff.

Ultimately, boards need to develop an approach to committee number, size, and purview that assures that: (i) each committee is serving its function; (ii) the system of selecting committee chairs is judged to be fair and equitable; (iii) the balance of what committees decide and what comes to the board for decision is appropriate; (iv) members not on a particular committee feel comfortable that it has done its work and reached an appropriate decision or recommendation; and (v) committees are neither assuming too much power nor running ahead of the board.

Recognizing the potential dangers of overdoing both the number and the level of involvement of committees, foundation boards are increasingly taking a minimalist approach to delegating its responsibility to subgroups, establishing only those committees judged to be absolutely necessary, and doing the remaining work of the board as a committee of the whole. A basic set of foundation board committees might include:

Executive Committee: Usually comprising board officers and committee chairs, this committee acts with the full legal authority of the full board between its meetings. It also may: review and approve the board's annual operational budget; monitor the work of the chief staff officer, conduct his/her annual performance review, and establish performance goals for the subsequent year; and provide the chief staff officer with ready access to a subset of the board.

Finance and Investment Committee: This committee ensures the continued financial health of the foundation by overseeing those processes and mechanisms through which its assets are safeguarded and invested, its finances are managed, and its financial operations audited (although many foundations elect to have a separate audit committee).

Governance Committee: This committee oversees the work of the board, developing standards and criteria for the operation of the entire board, board committees, and individual members. This includes monitoring operations and recommending strategies for improving them; monitoring the contributions of individual members and helping to increase their effectiveness; and nominating candidates to fill board vacancies.

Since grantmaking is what a foundation is all about, boards increasingly are eschewing the creation of separate program committees, opting instead to make program decisions at the board level, and using a "consent agenda" approach to approving slates of recommendations from the staff, discussing only those on which there are significant questions or conflicts of interest. If a program committee is established, it is important to assure that its review processes don't overly burden the staff, extend the duration of the overall review process, or intrude on staff roles and prerogatives.

Board Learning: Continuous learning is an integral element of a foundation board's efforts to remain informed, knowledgeable, and effective. For this reason, boards should develop formal learning agendas comprising regular and varied opportunities to be exposed to a diversity of ideas, issues, people, organizations, and settings. Learning opportunities that are well-conceived and carried out help make board members: (i) better stewards of the foundation's assets; (ii) more informed about the substantive topics that represent its funding agenda; (iii) more aware of important forces that shape the world in which it operates, and trends that influence the foundation's future directions; and (iv) better able to assess progress and use that information to improve the foundation's performance and enhance its impacts. Such opportunities inform not only board decisions, but also the questions they ask about effectiveness, impact, and outcomes, and the way in which they use answers to those questions to help the foundation do a better job.

The Quantity and Quality of Information: An important element in a board's capacity to learn is the information it receives from the staff and from other sources about foundation programs, finances, and operations, about the organizations with which the foundation partners to achieve its mission and goals, and about the world in which the foundation operates. Keeping boards informed is a difficult challenge for all involved: the staff, as it struggles to educate and inform the board without overburdening its members; and the board, as it struggles to select and digest the large amount of information it receives, from both internal and external sources.

Finding the balance between not enough and too much information is a challenge. While it is important that board members have the information they need to make informed decisions, they should not be overwhelmed. Overly thick board books are daunting for members and require a great deal of preparation on the part of the staff. As part of a board's effort to strengthen its effectiveness as a governing entity, it should develop criteria to guide what information it needs and wants, including guidance on the balance between materials about organizational issues, and provocative materials designed to stimulate thinking and learning among members.

Remaining Open to Outside Voices: There is an unfortunate tendency among foundations, as they mature, to gradually come to believe that all valuable information and wisdom resides "in the building," to close in on themselves, and to lose track of what is actually going on in the communities they exist to serve. Being truly responsive to community values implies constantly seeking out, and being open to, the broadest diversity of sources of information, knowledge, and experience within communities of interest.

Boards use a variety of mechanisms for obtaining outside perspectives, including site visits to communities, organizations, and programs related to foundation interests; board meetings in locations representative of those in which the foundation works; and panel discussions involving people whose perspectives and experiences are germane to foundation programs. Members of foundation boards generally appreciate the opportunity to hold board meetings away from the foundation's offices, seeing them as chances to have direct contact with people and organizations affected by, and working on, the issues being addressed by the foundation. While such "away" meetings are expensive in terms of money, staff preparation, and board member time, they are almost always worth it.

Learning About Other Funders: Foundation boards wish to have and need to have information about the level of attention being paid to issues by other funders, both public and private. Absent such information, they are being asked to make decisions concerning the allocation of significant resources to address specific issues, without knowing what other resources are being devoted to the area. This need is most often met through the inclusion, in every staff funding recommendation, of an analysis of the level of resources and attention being devoted to that issue by other funders.

The Views of Constituents: Foundation board members also wish to know more about how various constituencies feel about how the foundation is doing. This most often takes the form of a "customer satisfaction survey" to determine how the foundation is perceived by those who have been funded, those who have been turned down, and those who are ineligible to participate. The goal is to find out how the foundation is being perceived by external audiences, and to use that information to improve its programs and operations.

Evaluation of Foundation Programs: Accountability for the outcomes of funded programs is part of a foundation board's fiduciary responsibility, equal in importance to its accountability for asset management. For this reason, part of the information a board needs to be effective relates to progress, productivity, and impact of projects and programs, and performance of the foundation as a whole. Evaluation is a window on the value of a foundation's philanthropic activities, and serves as a basis for learning about what works and what doesn't. Ultimately, board members should be concerned less with the performance of individual grants than with what clusters of grants, programs, and the work of the foundation, as a whole, add up to in terms of progress toward achieving its goals and advancing its mission.

Making evaluation serve the purposes of learning and program improvement requires: (i) a clear board policy on the rationale for assessment, when and how it will be conducted, and how resulting information will be used; (ii) development, by the staff, of strategies for implementing the board's policy; and (iii) organizational structures and processes for analyzing and interpreting assessments, and for feeding the resulting information back to the foundation and its grantees in such a way as to facilitate its use in improving program funding and implementation.

Evaluation of Board Effectiveness: An integral part of a foundation's educational agenda should be regular assessments of its own performance, as a way of helping the board, as well as individual members, do a better job of governance. The first element of assessing board performance is looking at the board as a whole. This starts with the development of expectations, criteria, and standards for use in judging the performance of the board as a governing body. These help the board assess the degree to which it has, as a body: governed effectively; operated efficiently; met its goals; handled in a sensitive manner; and managed turnover with as little disruption as possible. This kind of assessment can involve regular internal reviews and assessments conducted by the governance committee (see above), supplemented by more in-depth processes of self-reflection facilitated by outside consultants.

The second element of board assessment is looking at the contributions of individual members. This can be accomplished through the development of performance criteria, standards, and measures for assessing the performance of board members individually, and the application of those measures fairly, equitably, and courageously to improving performance and dealing with members who are not pulling their weight. All boards, especially smaller ones, depend on the full engagement of all members. Every seat at the board table is critical and should be filled by someone who contributes. While not every director can contribute equally to all board deliberations and processes, there is a level of attendance, preparation, and engagement to which every member should be held accountable.

Chapter 7: Executive Management: Linking Policy and Action

KEY LINK AND INTEGRATIVE FORCE

The chief staff officer (CSO) of a foundation is the essential link between the board and the staff. The CSO stands at the crossroads of communications traffic among the board, the staff, and various external constituencies and sources: (i) translating board decisions into directions for staff action; and (ii) filtering, digesting, and summarizing for the board, information from the staff, and from others, on progress, outcomes, challenges, and opportunities.

Effective, organized philanthropy depends on integration of a spectrum of key elements, ranging from the lofty – philanthropic philosophy, societal needs, and foundation mission – to the mundane – grantmaking processes, budgets, operations, and staff performance reviews. In reality, only the CSO of a foundation is in a position to serve this integrative function. The board is comprised of individuals with a limited amount of time to devote to the foundation's business. The staff, while full time, is focused on assuring the effective day-to-day implementation of those particular programs or operations for which they are responsible. Only the CSO has the perspective, the information, the resources, and the leverage it takes to see the whole picture and understand how the foundation fits within it, to visualize the many aspects of philanthropy and understand how they all fit together, and to mobilize all of the foundation's assets in an integrated and coherent way to achieve maximum impact.

ROLES AND RESPONSIBILITIES

No matter the title – executive director, president, or president and CEO – a foundation's chief staff officer, like that of any other organization, is accountable to the governing board for executive management of the organization. This means:

- Leading and managing the foundation's programmatic, administrative, and financial units in such a way that each operates at full capacity, and that, collectively, they constitute an organization capable of achieving its mission and goals;

- Leading and managing the foundation's staff and overseeing its implementation of board decisions, and its adherence to policies, plans, and budgets approved by the board; and

- Promoting, facilitating, and sustaining the kinds of open, relevant, and informative communications a philanthropy depends on for its ultimate success – between the board and staff, among the staff, and between the foundation and the environment in which it operates.

Leading and Managing: Within this general organizational context, the CSO is responsible, specifically, for leading the foundation in the direction it needs to go in order to attain its ambitious philanthropic goals, and for managing the programs and operations it has established to get there. This means:

Maximizing Board Effectiveness – Facilitating and enhancing efforts by the foundation's board to carry out its governance roles in the most effective and responsible manner. An effective CSO is one who, while respecting board prerogatives and authority, sees members of the board as partners and allies in the foundation's efforts to maximize its assets and deploy them in such a way as to have the greatest impact. Accordingly, the CSO: (i) meets with each member of the board individually on a regular basis to establish and maintain a good working relationship, and to obtain his or her views on opportunities, challenges, and problems; (ii) provides the board with the information it needs to understand the principal issues it faces, to make informed decisions, to measure progress toward achievement of specific goals, and to assess the foundation's overall performance; (iii) strives to make meetings of the board and its committees as efficient, productive, and educational as possible, highlighting key issues and including a variety of learning opportunities; and (iv) responds to board questions and requests in a timely fashion.

Maximizing Staff Effectiveness – Developing and fully utilizing the asset represented by the foundation's staff. An effective foundation CSO gets the most out of a foundation's staff, by:

- Establishing recruitment, orientation, development, review, and reward systems that build and sustain a staff with high levels of commitment, passion, expertise, and productivity;

- Building a diverse staff who reflect the full range of perspectives the foundation needs to understand and address its mission and who work together in such a way that multiculturalism is one of the foundation's core strengths;

- Providing the staff with the information it needs to understand board decisions and actions, what is expected of them, and how their performance will be measured;

- Recognizing and acknowledging staff contributions and accomplishments, and providing opportunities for staff members to present directly to the board, as feasible and appropriate;

- Maximizing the amount of time staff members spend in the field gaining firsthand knowledge of community problems and resources, and minimizing the time they spend in the office pushing paper;

- Creating the time and space staff members need to stay current in their areas of expertise and foundation work, to learn new areas and skills, and to reflect on the work they are doing and on how it can be done better;

- Building and constantly strengthening the management team with which the CSO works in running the foundation, and on which the foundation would have to depend were something to happen to the CSO; and

- Encouraging and facilitating opportunities for staff members to interact socially among themselves, with management, and with the board.

Maximizing Organizational Effectiveness – Organizing and managing the foundation in such a way that its programs and operations fully serve, support, and advance its philanthropic mission and goals. An effective foundation CSO:

- Keeps the organization's eye on *The Prize*, focusing its resources, energies, and talents on achieving the goals it has established, on solving the problems it has chosen to address, and on helping the people it has selected for special attention;

- Works with each organizational unit to assure that it understands its role in the organization and fulfills that role as effectively as possible;

- Aligns and orchestrates the operations of all organizational units so that, they constitute an integrated institutional entity pursuing its goals in a coherent manner;

- Creates an environment that is conducive to the pursuit of philanthropic ends, values thinking, creativity, and collaboration, and is open to others' perspectives, opinions, and ideas; and

- Creates the time, space, and systems the foundation needs to assess the contributions of grants and programs, and the organization's overall performance, to extract the lessons learned, and to apply those lessons to improving what the foundation does and how it does it.

Maximizing Relationships With External Constituents – Stressing the degree to which the foundation's effectiveness and ultimate impact depends on the quality and productivity of its relationships with a broad range of outside constituents, including potential grantees, actual grantees, community leaders, policy-makers, government agencies, other foundations, and the media. An effective CSO creates an organizational culture that:

- Recognizes and values the potential contributions of all these constituents to achieving the foundation's mission and goals;

- Perceives nonprofit organizations as partners whose work is vital to the foundation's mission, and whose survival, integrity, and well-being are of utmost concern;

- Minimizes the bureaucratic hoops through which applicants must jump to obtain funding, and the hurdles over which grantees must jump to keep it, stressing substance over form, quality over quantity, performance over promise, and dialogue over paper;

- Establishes and enforces a code of conduct based on the golden rule, not the rule of gold; and

- Insists that all organizations be treated with respect, fairness, and equity, eschewing favoritism and minimizing conflicts of interest.

ATTRIBUTES OF EFFECTIVE CHIEF EXECUTIVES

Nothing about the roles and responsibilities outlined above should be a surprise; they are consistent with the general principles applied by a wide range of organizations in both the public and private sectors, especially those highly dependent upon external partners for their success. Yet, when it comes to hiring chief staff officers, foundations often pay only lip service to these principles, choosing high visibility, high name recognition, and sterling credentials over proven leadership and management capabilities. It's as though the board has come to believe that the foundation can best achieve its goals through rhetoric, fame, and public relations, rather than through the hard work that characterizes effective philanthropy. The following represent some of the attributes associated with effective executive management of foundations.

Clarity of Purpose: Some individuals are attracted to running a foundation because of their personal commitment to solving particular social issues or helping particular population groups. Others see foundation work as highly prestigious, socially valued, secure, and rewarding. While both rationales are understandable, they are not necessarily consistent with effective foundation executive management. It is certainly imperative that a foundation CSO be committed to philanthropy as a means of improving the human condition, and likely that he or she will be more attuned to certain social issues and/or population groups than to others. However, it is essential that a foundation CSO be able to distinguish between his or her private agenda and that of the foundation's, and to suppress the former. Given the roles and responsibilities outlined above, it must be clear that the CSO is not a free agent for whom the foundation is a vehicle for pursuing personal agendas, but the agent of the board to whom he or she reports, the leader of a staff that reports to him or her, and an advocate for the issues and communities the foundation exists to address. An effective foundation CSO is one who has the maturity and security it takes to devote full attention to advancing the work of the foundation, rather than using the foundation as a platform for personal advancement or aggrandizement.

Relevant Substantive Expertise: There are advantages to foundations being led by individuals who are generalists in terms of their substantive expertise. This is especially true for some of the larger foundations, which have broad interests and multiple programs. That said, among the qualifications a CSO brings to the job should be interests, knowledge, and expertise that relate directly to one or more of the foundation's areas of emphasis and the strategies it employs in pursuing them. There are several reasons for this preference. First, the CSO should either arrive with, or readily acquire, an understanding of the foundation's areas of focus, the special challenges posed by those areas, and the rationale underlying the foundation's approach to addressing them. Second, the CSO should be able to speak knowledgeably and articulately to a variety of audiences – both internal and external – about the foundation and its programs, and be able to respond to questions, criticisms, and challenges in a thoughtful way. Third, the CSO should know enough to be able to discuss programmatic issues with the staff, understand their triumphs, challenges, and frustrations, and provide helpful advice and guidance.

Leadership and Management Skills: Running a foundation of any size is first and foremost a job of leadership and management. Yes, philanthropy is about altruism, charity, and giving money to worthy organizations for important charitable work. But doing so in a way that maximizes the impact of the resources expended, the capacities and productivity of the organizations supported, the talent and abilities of the board and staff, the effectiveness and efficiency of the organization, and the fairness and integrity of the grantmaking processes employed requires skillful leadership and firm management.

Financial Acumen: Philanthropy is about money: managing it, accounting for it, and spending it for charitable purposes. Managing a foundation's assets involves balancing the desire to maximize resources through aggressive investment strategies with the need to protect and preserve capital over the long term, and to provide the cash needed to meet annual payout. Managing those assets also means development of and adherence to program and operational budgets. This is the area of philanthropy which is most highly regulated and carefully scrutinized by federal and state authorities. And finally, spending a foundation's resources for maximum impact also involves hard choices, strict discipline, and management skills.

While ultimate fiduciary responsibility rests with the board, it is the CSO who is responsible for assuring that those policies are adhered to by the staff and its external advisors and managers.

Accordingly, a foundation's chief staff officer must possess at least a fundamental interest in, and understanding of, investment and financial principles, know enough to be able to manage staff who are experts in these disciplines, and be sufficiently comfortable with that knowledge to be able to convince the board, and outside auditors, that the foundation's financial house is in good hands.

Communications Skills: Competent leadership and management involve excellent communications skills. Consistent with the linkage role described above, a foundation's CSO must be able to: (i) communicate with the board, providing them with the information they need to carry out their governance responsibilities and extracting from their discussions the essence of intended policies, decisions, and actions; (ii) communicate with the staff, giving them the essential information they need to translate board policies, decisions, and actions into reality, and extracting from their reports and observations critical information about successes, opportunities, problems, and challenges; and (iii) represent the foundation to a range of external constituencies and audiences, and convey back to the board and staff their views on the state of their world and how the foundation can make it better. Part of this skill involves a willingness to tell it as it is, to support unpopular or even controversial actions, and to take responsibility for decisions that inevitably disappoint or anger some constituents.

THE FRONT LINE OF PHILANTHROPY

Ultimately, a foundation pursues its mission through the support of nonprofit organizations which, in its view, have the potential to contribute the most to achieving its programmatic goals. Accordingly, at the end of the day, a foundation's success is dependent on the effectiveness of the processes through which it: (i) selects the organizations it funds; (ii) deploys its resources to support those organizations; (iii) monitors and assesses their work; and (iv) relates to them as partners in addressing compelling social challenges.

While the board establishes overall directions and policies, and the chief executive oversees their implementation, the front line in organized philanthropy is a foundation's program staff. It is they who design and carry out grant making programs established by the Board, and who constitute the foundation's principal face, voice, and agency in the communities in which it works. And it is the foundation's administrative and support staffs who carry out the myriad internal functions that make a foundation's programs productive. Chapter 4 will deal with the alignment and integration of a foundation's internal organizational units in which the critical grants management, communications, human resources, financial, and legal, functions are carried out. This chapter concerns itself with the program staff and how their effectiveness can be maximized.

An Asset to be Valued: The staff represents a core human resource which, to a large extent, determines the degree to which a foundation is successful in deploying its core financial resources. As such, the staff should be seen as an asset to be maximized, rather than a cost to be minimized. Just as a foundation manages its financial assets for maximum growth and return, so should it manage its human resources in such a way that they are maximally nurtured, developed, and used. To a surprising degree, organized philanthropy has devoted relatively little time and energy to refining and optimizing the processes through which foundation program staffs are selected, developed, nurtured, evaluated, and rewarded. A critical element in efforts to strengthen philanthropy's role in solving significant social problems is the development of improved strategies for:

- Defining the personal and professional attributes of individuals that make them effective program staff members;

- Attracting, recruiting, and selecting people who exhibit those attributes;

- Orienting new program staffers to the field of philanthropy and the nature of their work in that field;

- Documenting the factors that contribute to the performance of particularly effective program staff;

- Keeping program staff committed, engaged, in tune with reality, and effective;

- Assessing and rewarding performance; and

- Recognizing when the time is right for program staff members to move on, and helping them do so.

PROGRAM STAFF ROLES AND RESPONSIBILITIES

Organizational Context: Foundation staff members, like staffers of any organization, are responsible for implementing the activities through which the foundation achieves its desired ends, and for operating the organizational units through which it carries out its management, financial, human resource, legal, and other administrative and support functions. Foundation program staff are accountable to their chief executive for implementation of decisions by the foundation's board concerning program directions and policies. This means:

- Translating the rhetoric concerning where the foundation intends to go – as articulated in its mission and goals – into the reality of programs;

- Implementing board decisions concerning what the foundation intends to do programmatically, including program priorities, strategies, and style of operation;

- Implementing board policies governing how the foundation goes about achieving its goals;

- Assuring that the foundation's resources are allocated responsibly and prudently, and expended appropriately; and

- Providing the chief executive with the information she or he needs to: (i) be on top of what is going on; (ii) anticipate problems (no surprises, please!); (iii) make informed decisions; and (iv) keep the board informed.

Making It Happen: Within this general organizational context, the foundation program staff is responsible, specifically, for all aspects of the grantmaking and other activities through which the foundation pursues its programmatic aspirations. In the end, it is the program staff that makes it happen. This means:

Learning – Gaining as much knowledge as possible about: (i) the problems on which the foundation has decided to focus its attention and resources; (ii) the larger social, economic, political, and cultural contexts in which the problems exist; (iii) the people whose well-being the foundation hopes to enhance through its programs; (iv) the communities in which foundation programs are to be implemented; (v) the most accessible and potentially productive "levers of change" the foundation might push to achieve its goals; (vi) the individuals and organizations with which the foundation might partner; and (vii) the climate for success, including receptivity and readiness.

Program Design – On the basis of the knowledge gained during the learning process: (i) articulating clear program goals, expected outcomes, and milestones; (ii) specifying the parameters within which the program must operate, such as grantmaking dollars, time, and staff input; (iii) identifying alternative strategies through which the program can achieve its goals, consistent with those parameters; (iv) selecting those program strategies judged to have the greatest potential for success; and (v) incorporating those strategies into a coherent, systematic effort by the foundation to deploy all the resources at its command to advance the causes to which it is committed.

Grantee Selection – Identifying potential organizations with whom the foundation might partner in pursuit of its program goals, and selecting those judged to have the greatest potential for success. This involves solicitation, review, and decision-making processes that are not only effective and efficient from the foundation's view, but fair, equitable, timely, and minimally burdensome and intrusive from the perspective of applicant organizations.

Due Diligence – Implementing those review, selection, and oversight mechanisms and processes required to assure, to the degree possible, that: (i) grants are awarded to organizations capable of achieving their stated goals, and of administering them in a responsible manner; and (ii) grant funds are expended in accordance with the terms of the agreement through which they were awarded. This "due diligence" is the responsibility of the staff. For while foundation boards ultimately decide what to fund and what not to, they must rely on the judgment of the staff concerning applicants' programmatic and administrative capacities, and grantees' program performance and financial responsibility.

Program Management – Undertaking those actions necessary to increase a program's potential for success by (i) coordinating and integrating the various elements of a program to assure that "all the moving parts" are aligned and complementary; (ii) facilitating the work of grantees, as feasible and appropriate, through the support of technical assistance, advice, and capacity-building; (iii) using the foundation's convening power, communications expertise and resources, contacts with other funders, and other assets and capacities to advance, leverage, and extend the work of grantees; and (iv) linking and networking grantees so that, to the degree possible, their collective work is greater than the sum of their individual efforts.

Improving – Closing the loop by (i) maintaining knowledge and awareness of the context in which foundation programs are operating, and of any changes that may influence how those programs progress and succeed; (ii) monitoring the work of grantees through written reports, regular contact, and visits; (iii) assessing the degree to which foundation grants and grantmaking programs are achieving their goals; (iv) extracting lessons from this information; and (v) using those lessons to strengthen the work of grantees and improve all aspects of the foundation's programmatic performance.

CONDUCT AND BEHAVIOR

These roles and responsibilities constitute a significant challenge for foundation staff. Fulfilling them in a way that maximizes the effectiveness of the foundation's programs and operations means that they must:

- Understand the obligations they have to the foundation's governing board, partners, and constituents to keep their individual and collective eyes on *The Prize* as articulated in the foundation's mission, and to operate always in a way that is fair, equitable, and transparent;

- Treat all individuals and organizations with whom the foundation comes in contact with respect and dignity, recognizing that it is through them that the foundation achieves its ends, and avoiding the arrogance, elitism, and isolation that comes to characterize so many of us who have power and money that others lack;

- Balance personal beliefs and agendas with the foundation's mission, and with their responsibility to protect the integrity of the foundation's operational processes;

- Understand that, while they bring to the foundation their perspectives on particular racial or ethnic minorities, social or economic classes, age cohorts, or geographic areas, they do not represent those groups as though they were constituents;

- Operate in a trusting, cohesive, and collegial manner, so that the whole of the foundation's programs and operations is greater than the sum of its individual organizational units;

- Respect the roles, responsibilities, and prerogatives of the board, striving toward a relationship characterized by mutual trust, respect, and collegiality, and communicating with directors primarily through the chief staff officer;

- Adhere to a policy of strict confidentiality concerning all foundation discussions, actions, decisions, and materials; and

- Recognize and deal with actual, potential, or apparent conflicts of interest promptly and openly (See Appendix B for a model conflict of interest policy and disclosure form).

ATTRIBUTES OF EFFECTIVE PROGRAM STAFF

Despite the critical importance of program staff to the work of foundations, there is little collective wisdom in the field of philanthropy about what makes for an effective program staff member, how to identify individuals who are likely to be successful in that role, and how to assess their performance once they are hired. Accordingly, recruitment and selection of program staff is often hit and miss, with many individuals who look good on paper and interview well not living up to expectations, and with others who appear unsuited for the job performing admirably. And performance review, incentive, and reward systems in philanthropy are often so poorly thought out and implemented that they may actually encourage behavior opposite to that desired. That said, there are some things we have learned about what to look for in recruiting people to become program staff members, and what criteria to apply in assessing their performance.

Commitment to the Foundation's Mission: Program staff should demonstrate a genuine interest in the work of the foundation, and view working there as an opportunity to contribute to the fulfillment of its mission. While altruism isn't sufficient for success, it represents a core value that goes a long way in helping program staff succeed in a world where rewards are ephemeral. Too often, individuals are drawn to philanthropy because they perceive it to be a respite from the hectic demands of the "real world," a secure place to do highly prestigious work without working too hard. After all, giving away money is easy, isn't it?

Personal Maturity and Security: Successful program staff members are secure in who they are, professionally and personally, obviating the need for them to build themselves up at the expense of others. Internally, it is important for program staff to remember, always, that they are not independent agents, but staff to a board that sets directions and makes final decisions concerning allocation of the foundation's resources, and part of an organization in which all parts are equal and must work together in harmony if its mission is to be attained. Externally, there is always the danger in philanthropy for abuse of the intrinsic imbalance of power between foundations that have money and applicants who want some of it, or grantees who want more of it. There is nothing that undermines the relationship between foundations and their constituencies more than the arrogance of program staff who fall prey to the self-delusions that often characterize those with power.

Breadth of Interests: There is a tension in any foundation between hiring program staff with specialized expertise and talent and those with broader interests and capacities. The tendency among most foundations is toward the latter, for several reasons. First, the kinds of problems addressed by foundations don't lend themselves to narrow, single-dimensional approaches.

Second, foundations increasingly recognize the degree to which societal problems are interconnected, often linked to many of the same underlying causes. Third, there is growing exploration within philanthropy of new organizational models designed to facilitate collaboration among staff, and between staff and grantees, in addressing complex challenges. And, fourth, foundations may change their programmatic directions in response to the need to stay focused on what are perceived to be the most important problems in the communities they serve. All these reasons lead many in the field to conclude that effective program staffers are those who have broad interests and knowledge, intellectual curiosity, ability to learn quickly, and a flexible nature.

Problem-Solving Orientation: At the its core, foundation program work involves deploying philanthropic dollars to contribute to the solution of societal problems. Accordingly, effective program staffers are those who: (i) are animated by that challenge; (ii) recognize the magnitude and complexity of those problems; and (iii) have the vision, capacity, and persistence to systematically analyze their roots, identify potentially productive points of intervention, and develop programs designed to exploit those points of intervention in the most effective way. Philanthropy, at its best, is characterized by individuals who have literally changed the world through their focused, systematic, intensive (some would say "single-minded"), and strategic efforts to solve a problem affecting the health or well-being of large numbers of people.

Comfort With Vicarious Rewards: Philanthropy, by its very nature, involves providing the resources others need to achieve their work. It is those others who will be directly involved in addressing the problem, delivering the services, and helping people. And it is those others who will – and should – get the credit for what is accomplished. Foundation program staff support, enable, and facilitate the work leading to those accomplishments, but they do so invisibly and behind the scenes. The most effective foundation program staffers are those who understand and embrace this role, who get their kicks out of helping make it possible for others to do good work, and who always give credit where credit is due.

Comfort With Ambiguity: Trying to change the world is not work for the faint of heart. Because of the imbalance between the resources of even the largest foundations and the magnitude of the social problems they exist to address, foundations seek to focus their attention on problems that, in their judgment, are especially critical for the populations they serve, and relatively neglected by others. That means that those problems are likely to be particularly complex, difficult to tackle, and, perhaps, even controversial or unattractive. As a consequence, progress in addressing the problem is slow, hard work, difficult to measure, and virtually impossible to attribute to the foundation's efforts.

If assessing the impact of a foundation program is elusive, imagine the challenge of trying to assess the contributions of an individual program staff member to that program. In fact, the field of philanthropy has yet to address systematically the problem of how to evaluate the performance of program staff. Lacking criteria related to program effectiveness, supervisors often resort to mundane, bureaucratic measures of performance, such as the quality of written documents, the timeliness of responding to inquiries or proposals, and the degree to which files are kept up to date. As a result, the system actually rewards staff who spend their time at their desk moving paper, rather than out in the field where the action is. The lack of clear indicators of performance and resulting perversity of the reward system make it difficult for program staffers to know how they're doing in the eyes of their supervisors, and create a level of ambiguity that undermines staff effectiveness and morale.

Listening Ear: There is no single or simple solution to the kinds of problems foundations face. Progress in addressing them depends on a systematic analysis of their roots, exploration of the many alternative strategies for achieving the desired change, and implementation of those judged to be the most likely to be effective. It follows, then, that no single person has the answer. Each step of this process requires identification of people who understand the problem and its consequences, know about its roots, have experience with other efforts to solve the problem, and have ideas about how to do it better. Effective program staff are constantly listening and learning, identifying key informants, building confidence that their opinions matter, maintaining a listening ear and an open mind, and incorporating what they hear into their thinking, their program designs, their implementation strategies, and their style of operation. Close-minded individuals who tend to think they have all the answers are antithetical to effective philanthropy.

Collaborative Style: Effective philanthropy increasingly is a collaborative venture. Making a difference in the kinds of social arenas in which foundations work requires the involvement of, and interaction among, a range of partners, including: (i) grantee organizations; (ii) community leaders; (iii) other foundations; (iv) policy-makers; (v) government agencies; and (vi) colleagues within the same foundation. Accordingly, program staffers need to embrace this collective style of operation and to have personalities that are consistent with the kind of collaboration that benefits all involved, equally.

ENHANCING AND SUSTAINING STAFF EFFECTIVENESS

These characteristics and practices don't just happen, and, once they are achieved, don't automatically endure. In fact, the very independence and self-sufficiency that create the opportunity for foundation staff to apply their talents to the solution of important social problems may produce an organizational environment in which those capacities are difficult to sustain. That environment can generally be characterized by:

Comfort – Pleasant surroundings, relatively generous compensation and benefits, adequate support staff and services, job security, and the satisfaction that derives from being involved in socially beneficial causes; and

Insulation – Freedom from the need to raise money, be accountable to shareholders, politicians, or political constituencies; distance from the day-to-day exigencies and immediacy of directly dealing with the consequences of the social problems the foundation is trying to solve; and protection from the truth, seldom receiving honest feedback from individuals or organizations, many of whom are grantees or wish to be.

Within such an environment, there is the constant danger that program staff will become "stuck" – complacent, out of touch with reality, and stale – and that the programs for which they are responsible will become pedestrian, safe, and reactive. Accordingly, a major challenge facing foundations is to create and institutionalize processes and mechanisms designed to keep its program staff productive, vital, and fresh. Meeting that task is sufficiently important and difficult that it requires the deliberate and thoughtful development, implementation, and evaluation of specific policies and programs.

Policy Framework: The ultimate success of a foundation's effort to sustain its staff's creativity, openness, objectivity, and future orientation depends upon the formulation and implementation of a set of policies that have broad support at all levels of the organization, and are coherent, comprehensive, explicit, feasible, and appropriate. The effectiveness of policies directed toward the goal of sustaining staff performance and vitality depends upon the degree to which board members, managers, and staff recognize the importance of that goal and support efforts to attain it. Accordingly, it is critical that a consensus be developed among those groups that: (i) staff represent a significant foundation asset; (ii) the foundation's ultimate impact depends upon nurturing and sustaining staff vitality; and (iii) there is need for explicit policies and practices aimed at advancing that goal.

Policies directed toward promoting and sustaining staff vitality must be:

- *Comprehensive* – Encompassing the full spectrum of interactions between the foundation and its program staff, from recruitment to outplacement;

- *Coherent* – Constituting a consistent, integrated organizational commitment;

- *Feasible* – Fostering programs and activities that are consonant with the realities of the foundation's structure and operating style, and of the staff's obligations and duties; and

- *Appropriate* – Customizing programs and activities to particular needs of individual program staff members.

Ultimately, policies on staff productivity and vitality must become explicit, integral elements of the policy framework with which the foundation operates, and of the style that characterizes that operation, influencing a broad spectrum of judgments, decisions, and actions.

Policy Implementation: Policies consistent with these criteria constitute a framework within which efforts designed specifically to sustain the vitality and freshness of program staff can be developed, implemented, and evaluated. Such efforts relate to a series of opportunities for interaction between the foundation and its program staff aimed at assessing and influencing the individual's growth, development, and performance, and should be perceived, formulated, and carried out as a conscious, coherent, and integrated program of staff development.

Recruitment – It starts at the beginning: Everything is easier if a foundation is able to recruit individuals who are most likely to become and remain good program staff members. This means carefully developing its own list of the attributes it thinks are most critical to the success of program staff, and applying those criteria consistently in assessing the suitability of prospective hirees. In addition to the kinds of attributes described above, such criteria should include, to the degree possible, indicators of the capacity of potential staff members to remain vital and fresh. These might include measures of the degree to which they: (i) are driven by the desire to improve the human condition and impatient with the status quo; (ii) see foundations as critical instruments of change, rather than comfortable places to work in, or retire to; and (iii) are open to, and actively seeking, personal and professional learning and growth opportunities.

Orientation – Few come prepared for foundation work. There are no proven training programs, no logical career paths, no comparable work settings, and relatively little movement of staff among foundations. New staffers generally come from outside the field and are hired for their substantive expertise, not for their knowledge of philanthropy or their experience in grantmaking. It is assumed that they will learn on the job, so we throw them into the deep end of foundation work and let them sink or swim on their own.

Having recruited individuals judged to have the capacity to contribute to achievement of a foundation's programmatic goals, it only makes sense to increase the probability of their success by providing access to an orientation program designed to accelerate the rate at which they learn what they need to know to do their jobs most effectively. The content of an orientation agenda for new program staff might include:

- *Philanthropy 101* – The essence of philanthropic philosophy and behavior; its role in, and contributions to, our society; its relation to other major societal sectors and institutions; its strengths, weaknesses, and pitfalls;

- *Foundations as Organized Instruments of Philanthropy* – The evolution of philanthropy from individual giving to organized institution; foundations as legal entities; their resources and assets; their distinctive opportunities and obligations; the nature of their accountability; how they operate;

- *Grantmaking* – The nature of grants and their core role in achieving philanthropic goals; the system through which grants are developed, processed, awarded, and monitored; the role of program staff in each step; best practices; worst practices, traps, and pitfalls;

- *This Foundation* – The history of the foundation in which the new staff are working; the origins of its financial assets; its mission, interest areas, and substantive boundaries; its organizational structure, modus operandi, and style; what distinguishes it from other foundations;

- *Program Staff* – How the program staff are organized and operate; expectations concerning the relationship between program staff and various external constituencies; expectations concerning the relationship between program staff and other internal organizational units and the board; and

- *Human Resource Issues* – How the foundation perceives its staff and their roles in the organization; goal-setting and performance review philosophy and process; opportunities and processes for advancement and promotions; opportunities for growth and development; and the foundation's expectations concerning how long one should work there.

The strategy for conveying information about these topics might include the following elements:

- *Written Materials* – A compendium – staff manual – of information concerning the foundation and its programs, policies, structure, and modus operandi;

- *Readings* – Books, chapters, and articles about philanthropy and the issues faced by grantmakers;

- *Seminars* – Discussions with foundation staff and guests about issues, challenges, and controversies in philanthropy, and organized grantmaking; and

- *Mentoring* – Pairing new staff with more senior colleagues who can help ease their entry into foundation work, accelerate their learning process, and help them avoid the usual mistakes of newcomers to the field.

Ongoing Opportunities for Growth and Development: Once new staff have been exposed to an orientation program designed to ease the process of assimilation, there need to be in place ongoing opportunities for continued staff growth, development, and intellectual stimulation, provided within or outside the walls of the foundation.

The Staff Development Plan – Each staff member should participate in the preparation of a personalized plan for his or her ongoing growth and development, including: (i) identification of specific interests, needs, and weaknesses to be addressed; (ii) goals; (iii) strategies for achieving them; (iv) time frame; and (v) estimated costs (time and money). Such a plan should serve as a blueprint by staff and their managers for strategies to keep staff members stimulated and vital, and both should be held accountable for their implementation. Too often, staff development plans represent good intentions that are forgotten, neglected, or pushed aside by the exigencies of everyday work and budget limitations.

Internal Staff Development Opportunities – There are many internal mechanisms through which a foundation can provide ongoing opportunities for staff to be challenged. These include:

- *Continuing Education* – A program of educational programs, carried out by and within the foundation, designed to expose program staff to philosophical, political, substantive, strategic, and procedural issues in philanthropy and grantmaking.

- *Exposure to Ideas and People* – Regular opportunities to expose staff to new ideas and concepts by assuring a steady flow of intellectually exciting people through the foundation's doors. This can involve taking advantage of the many visitors to a foundation each year, imposing on them to participate in staff seminars and to meet with interested staff. In addition, foundations can institute visiting scholars programs intended to bring in, for longer periods of time, individuals capable of contributing to the organization's thinking and work on particular topics or issues.

- *Position Enrichment or Change* – At some point, all program staffers will reach a point at which their learning curve is flat, their creativity blunted, their objectivity compromised, and their productivity reduced. Among the strategies for preventing and combating such staleness are job enrichment, promotion, and job rotation.

   JOB ENRICHMENT: Enriching one's existing job may, in some cases, be the most effective and least disruptive strategy, for both an individual and the organization, to provide the opportunities and challenges needed to renew a program staff member's excitement and vitality. Options include: (i) changing the substantive focus of the programs in which the individual is involved; (ii) enlarging the substantive scope of work for which the individual is responsible; (ii) assigning the individual responsibility for exploring new programmatic directions and strategies, or other special projects; and (iv) increasing the financial and human resources over which the individual has control.

PROMOTION: Since upward movement within an organization is a way to force growth, advancement within a foundation is one key strategy for keeping staff challenged. Accordingly, as part of their staff development policies and practices, foundations should seek to provide opportunities for staff to move into positions of greater responsibility and reach, if and when such moves are judged to be beneficial to both the staff member and the organization. The potential for such advancement is both an inducement and reward for excellent performance; its judicious implementation not only helps retain and stimulate top staff, but also opens positions for others moving into or up the organization.

JOB ROTATION: A change of job assignment – even a horizontal one – may be just the ticket for someone not interested in vertical movement within the organization, but in need of change. Job rotation represents the kind of change in purview, shake up, reduction in comfort level, and introduction of new substantive and administrative challenges that forces one to form new ideas, explore new strategies, and deal with a whole new set of people and organizations.

External Staff Development Opportunities – Complementing these internal mechanisms for keeping staff fresh are opportunities for involvement in extracurricular activities – active participation in the oversight or operation of organizations of the kind the foundation supports, sabbaticals, and educational opportunities.

- *Involvement With NonProfit Organizations* – Involvement with organizations actively engaged with addressing problems such as those to which the foundation is committed: (i) brings the individual face-to-face with those problems and their consequences; (ii) puts the individual in a position where being from the foundation carries no weight; (iii) injects a mild dose of humility; (iv) provides a view of what struggling nonprofits go through on a day-to-day basis; and (v) sustains a sense of the real. Within the constraints of conflict of interest and availability of time, foundations should encourage their staff to engage in such activities, and facilitate involvement by paying any associated expenses, and permitting necessary and reasonable time off. Examples include: service on boards of nonprofit organizations; membership on advisory panels, review groups, and steering committees; volunteer work; and fundraising.

- *Brief Sabbaticals* – An extension of the concept of exposing staff to external challenges and realities is to encourage them to pursue opportunities to spend more extensive periods of time away from the foundation. Such brief sabbaticals (three months or so) would be designed to achieve specific purposes, including working for a nonprofit organization full time, spending time in another foundation, working with a policy-maker or government agency, studying a new area of potential foundation interest, or learning a new technique or skill. These opportunities would not be automatic, frequent, or granted lightly, but rather, sought after and competitive.

- *Educational Opportunities* – Other external opportunities for growth involve the pursuit of additional formal education and advanced degrees. Recognizing the value to the individual and the organization of further education, in terms of knowledge, expertise, credibility, and self-esteem, many foundations have extremely generous educational benefits, including time off, and tuition reimbursement plans.

Performance Evaluation: Although effective staff development requires constant attention, the annual performance evaluation process represents a time and a mechanism for reflecting on staff members' productivity and vigor, assessing their need for revitalization, and considering alternative opportunities for growth. In a sense, this annual process represents the principal formal vehicle through which the foundation's staff development policies become expressed and implemented. Accordingly, staff development should be an explicit element of that process, providing a framework within which agreement can be reached on development goals, appropriate growth opportunities, and reasonable benchmarks.

Exit Strategy: In instances where a staff member's interest, contributions, or freshness wanes, and efforts to create appropriate growth opportunities fail, outplacement may represent the most constructive staff development strategy for both the individual and the foundation. In such cases, the foundation should be prepared actively to assist the staff member in finding a more suitable situation, providing the requisite time, resources, and professional help. In fact, it may prove beneficial for the two parties to work together on the development of an exit strategy, well before it becomes necessary. There is a great deal of discussion within philanthropy about the degree to which it represents a career rather than an a career step. This reflects a concern about the impacts, on both the individual and the organization, of working too long in an environment that can be so protected, insular, and comparatively "cushy." The best thing for an individual, the foundation in which he or she works, and for the field may be for program staff not to spend extended periods of time in any one foundation, but to move in and out of the field, mixing philanthropy with experiences closer to the social problems of interest and concern.

Chapter 9: Organizing for Maximum Impact

ORGANIZATION MATTERS

A key element in effective philanthropy is alignment and integration of a foundation's organization so that every structure and every function contributes to achievement of the foundation's mission and goals. This must seem self-evident to those not familiar with the world of philanthropy. However, within that world, relatively little attention is paid to how best to organize for maximum philanthropic impact. This lack of attention to organizational structure and function can be attributed, at least in part, to: (i) the natural inclination of foundations to focus on substantive directions, priorities, and programs, rather than on what may be perceived to be more mundane organizational issues; (ii) the need for new foundations to get up and running as quickly as possible in order to meet payout requirements, postponing issues of structure and function for later – often much later; (iii) the fact that foundations tend to attract and recruit individuals more interested in social change than in institutional structure and processes; and (iv) the tendency for each foundation to believe that it is so "unique" that it has little to learn from other foundations or from organizations outside of philanthropy.

Accordingly, foundations often evolve with little thought to how they should be structured and operated to align with philanthropic mission and goals, optimize performance, and maximize impact. As a result, organizations that ought to be models of coherence, nimbleness, flexibility, responsiveness, and transparency, are too often overly fragmented, bureaucratic, rigid, unresponsive, and opaque. Not only does this lack of organizational alignment and integration impair foundations' effectiveness and impact, it also serves as a barrier to open and productive interactions with the very constituencies they exist to serve.

MAKING THE ORGANIZATION WORK

While issues of program design and strategy are what most motivate, excite, and preoccupy a foundation's board and staff, the effectiveness and efficiency of its day-to-day operations are often what determine the degree to which it is able to attain its ambitious goals and plans. Accordingly, issues of organizational design and operational strategy must receive a substantial level of ongoing attention. The following represent some of the issues that should be addressed as a foundation's board and staff strive for optimum performance and maximum impact.

Organizational Alignment: Just as foundations must keep their eyes on *The Prize* when designing their philanthropic programs, so should they remember their raison d'etre when designing their organizational structure and modus operandi. This means each organizational unit should be designed for, committed to, and held accountable for, maximizing the foundation's philanthropic impact.   Operationally, this means that: (i) every policy, process, and procedure is formulated and implemented to facilitate and expedite the foundation's philanthropic programs and activities; (ii) flexibility, accessibility, and responsiveness win out over bureaucracy and delay every time; and (iii) performance criteria, measures, incentives, and rewards are created and implemented as a means of assuring the sustained attention of each operational unit to aligning with philanthropic mission, to facilitating program implementation, and to minimizing bureaucratic impediments.

The following paragraphs describe the implications of these principles for some typical organizational units in foundations, with the exception of program staff, whose roles and responsibilities are described in Chapter 8.

Grants Management – Foundations with significant grantmaking activities often create a staff unit dedicated to managing the processes through which grant applications are solicited, received, processed, awarded, and monitored. The purpose of such a unit is to facilitate and accelerate the processing of large volumes of inquiries, proposals and grants, especially for those foundations in which unsolicited proposals represent a substantial portion of their portfolio. A second purpose is to protect program staff from the burdens associated with managing the administrative aspects of these transactions, freeing them to dedicate the greatest portion of their time and energy to substantive, programmatic activities.   In order to fulfill these purposes, it is necessary that a foundation's grants management staff develop:

- Consistent criteria and efficient mechanisms for handling inquiries, and for screening out grant applications that fall outside a foundation's areas of interest or do not meet its minimum requirements for funding;

- Mechanisms for logging in, acknowledging, and directing to the right program staff, letters of intent and full applications that pass through the initial screen;

- Strategies for expediting the awarding of approved grants;

- Mechanisms for logging in, acknowledging the receipt of, and directing to the right program staff, progress and final grant reports, and for requesting reports not submitted on time;

- Efficient, user-friendly electronic data systems for tracking inquiries, letters of intent, grant applications, grants, and reports, and for producing reports capable of capturing essential data and trends; and

- Open, trusting, and productive working relationships and communications channels with the program, financial, and legal staffs with whom they must work in order to carry out their roles effectively.

Communications – A foundation's communications staff has the responsibility for establishing and maintaining the channels and mechanisms through which foundation staff interact and share information among themselves, and through which the foundation communicates with various external audiences and constituencies. Internal communication is critical to the organization's smooth functioning, as it increases the degree to which all staff have access to a common body of information and knowledge, and to each other. Increasingly, external communication is seen as an integral element of a foundation's efforts to pursue its mission and achieve its programmatic goals. Through various communication strategies, a foundation can: (i) complement its grantmaking programs with campaigns aimed at raising public awareness about important issues affecting their well-being; (ii) provide technical assistance aimed at helping grantee organizations be more sophisticated in the way in which they use communications to achieve their goals; (iii) elicit the views of the communities it aims to serve through its programs; (iv) establish relationships among a diversity of organizations and institutions with which the foundation must work in order to achieve its goals; (v) draw attention to, and mobilize action on, issues, problems, and situations it believes represent major societal threats and challenges; and (vi) highlight the work of its grantees and of the problems on which they are working. To be maximally effective, staff responsible for the design and implementation of communications activities aimed at achieving these kinds of objectives must work hand in hand with the program staff most directly involved in the issues being addressed.

Human Resources: The human resources function within a foundation serves to establish and carry out policies and processes related to people – recruitment, retention, retirement, and outplacement; compensation and benefits; performance review and promotions; interpersonal conflicts; and internal communications. Fulfilling this function in a way that advances a foundation's mission means developing and implementing: (i) recruitment strategies designed to identify and attract people whose backgrounds, experience, interests, goals, and reward structures suit them for philanthropic work; (ii) orientation programs designed to bring new staff rapidly up to speed on the essentials of philanthropy, foundations as institutions, and the nature of grantmaking, and on the programmatic, organizational, and operational characteristics of the foundation for which they are coming to work; (iii) job categories, promotion criteria, performance appraisal systems, and compensation policies that recognize the activities and attributes of effective grantmakers, and reward their work without necessarily requiring the assumption of greater administrative responsibilities; and (iv) strategies designed to keep foundation staff "fresh."

Finance: Because foundations achieve their missions primarily through the transfer of money to grantees, finances figure into every facet of grantmaking, from application to final report. Accordingly, in addition to their responsibilities for asset and financial management, foundation financial staff are in a position either to facilitate or impede the organization's grantmaking activities. They can facilitate grantmaking by developing and implementing financial application and reporting requirements and procedures that are designed to ease the work of both foundation program staff and grantee administrators, and the establishment and maintenance of an effective working relationship between them.   Specifically, in collaboration with program and grants management staffs, they should: (i) develop budget formats for grant applications that are simple, easily understood and filled out, and minimally burdensome; (ii) require only those financial documents that are absolutely necessary for analysis of the applicant organization's financial health; (iii) make grant payments on a schedule that is convenient to grantees, appropriate to the work they have proposed to carry out, and consistent with their financial situations, rather than on one driven by what is convenient for the foundation; (iv) permit maximum flexibility in how grantees expend the funds they have been awarded to achieve the goals of the grant, rather than adhering to arbitrary and rigid formulae and thresholds; (v) develop financial reporting requirements and forms that seek only the essential information needed to determine how the foundation's funds were expended; and (vi) reduce the amount of time program staff devote to financial matters by assisting them with the analysis of budgets and reports.

Legal: Legal considerations enter into many aspects of a foundation's operations. On the non-program side, these include asset management, real estate, taxes, employment, risk management, and contracting with vendors. On the program side, a foundation's legal counsel – whether internal, external, or a combination of the two – plays an important role in structuring the relationships and transactions through which the organization pursues its grantmaking goals. In many situations faced by program staff as they attempt to create and exploit programmatic opportunities, there are legal ramifications that have to do with what is permissible under various federal and state laws and regulations, and with what is best for the foundation. In these situations, counsel can either see itself as facilitating the foundation's programmatic activities through the work of the program staff, or as the organization's legal watchdog, avoiding risk at all costs. At a minimum, counsel should: (i) structure grant award documents in such a way as to provide grantees with maximum latitude within reasonable limits; (ii) facilitate the development of creative organizational arrangements needed for collaborations among private funders, between private funders and public entities, and between funders and grantee organizations; and (iii) interpret laws and regulations concerning issues such as advocacy in such a way as to help the foundation achieve its mission, rather than adopting a legal position that is so rigid as to preclude it from using many potentially useful strategies.

Organizational Integration: As important as alignment of a foundation's organizational units is to achievement of its mission, the degree to which those separate units are integrated into a coherent functional whole is fundamental to ultimate performance and impact. It is critical that, in addition to each organizational unit carrying out its duties in a way that facilitates and supports programmatic goals and activities, they work together so that, collectively, they represent a smoothly operating, collaborative organism whose eyes are on *The Prize* of making a difference in the lives of the people it exists to serve. Keys to such organizational integration include: (i) management that leads the organization much as a conductor leads an orchestra; (ii) mutual trust and respect among staff of the various organizational units that must work together to make the foundation successful; (iii) hiring, performance review, and compensation practices that stress, recognize, and reward "integrative" behavior; and (iv) internal communication channels and vehicles that facilitate access among all staff to critical information about the foundation and its programs, and ease of interaction among staff throughout the organization.

Epilogue

In looking back at what one has written, there is the tendency to ask: "Who cares?" My answer, in this case, is that we'd better all care – all of us who recognize the distinctive and significant roles individual and organized philanthropy play in American society and around the world. We should care because the independence that confers on foundations their comparative advantage as agents of social improvement makes them vulnerable to the exigencies of political and economic processes. For it is the government – federal and state – that, through its laws and regulations, permits and protects that independence, and, as we know, those who give may also take away! And who is there to speak up for the interests of this unusual societal institution?

I am reminded of this fact as I send this manuscript off to the publisher, because, as I write, we are embroiled once again in a public policy debate about whether foundations are contributing enough of their protected largesse to supporting worthy causes. The issue is whether foundations should be permitted to continue to count their administrative costs toward their annual 5% distribution. But it could be any number of questions related to how foundations should bear more of the burden of helping today's most needy. The economy is shaky; the polity is increasingly conservative; taxes are anathema; the federal government is reducing its support of social programs; and the states are almost all running large deficits. As a result, nonprofit agencies are feeling the pinch, cutting their budgets, staffs, and services. Safety net providers are barely surviving, school years are being cut short as districts run out of money. States are increasingly turning to gambling for revenue, and cities are struggling to provide even the most basic services. It is at times like this that foundations are particularly vulnerable. Social activists, commentators, and politicians see the amount of money represented by foundation endowments and wonder if enough of those resources are being applied to helping support important social purposes, and if foundations are doing enough to deserve their special status.

Whatever the outcome of this current debate, it is characteristic of the kind of controversy constantly swirling around foundations as they attempt to attend to their philanthropic knitting. And it reminds us that foundations can never rest on their laurels, never feel satisfied that, after all, they are "doing God's work," and never stop striving to reach *The Prize* – the missions which they were established to pursue. This means:

- Demonstrating, convincingly, that their significant contributions to the betterment of society warrant the continuation of the special legal and financial status that permits them to go where others can't; anticipate emerging issues before others perceive them to be problems; take the long view in addressing those issues; and experiment with solutions that others haven't thought of, or are unable or afraid to try;

- Staying focused on priority issues, avoiding drift, diffusion of purpose, and fatigue, and the tendency to placate constituents by spreading grant money so thinly among them that it accomplishes little or nothing;

- Developing creative and effective strategies for establishing realistic goals toward which foundations should strive, and metrics for determining the degree to which they are being achieved;

- Constantly reflecting, evaluating, learning, and sharing lessons with others in a way that: assures continuous improvement of foundation programs and operations; helps grantees strengthen their organizations and programs; and contributes to the accumulation of a body of knowledge and experience in the field of philanthropy on which foundation staff and boards can draw when designing their organizations and programs;

- Treating all with whom they come into contact with dignity and respect, avoiding the arrogance and isolation that too often creeps into relationships characterized by an imbalance of power; and

- Looking systematically at how foundations are governed and operated; optimizing the functioning of the board, executive management, and staff; and aligning and integrating organizational units so that they not only operate effectively and efficiently, but support and complement each other so as to advance the organization's overall mission and goals.

This is an ambitious set of principles to which foundations must adhere if they are to deserve the continued special and valued status in today's environment. But adhere to them they must.

Appendix A: Conflicts of Interest Policy for Foundation Board Members

CONTEXT AND OBLIGATIONS

In considering one's obligations as a foundation board member, it is important to understand the special public status of the foundation and its accompanying obligations.

Foundations are accorded the privileges of a public trust, based on the assumption that they will optimize use of their tax-exempt resources in the public's direct interest. The burden of proof is on foundations to demonstrate that they are meeting this standard and, therefore deserve the continuing privileges of their protected status.

As stewards of a public trust, board members are expected to establish and maintain standards of fairness, as well as meet their specific fiduciary responsibilities. When entering into financial transactions with business enterprises and vendors, the overriding obligation of boards is to protect their foundation's financial position. In distributing foundation resources to the community in the form of grants, the overriding obligation of the board is to protect the foundation's credibility, integrity, and fairness in dealing with the issues it addresses, and the grantee communities and organizations with which it partners. This requires that the actions board members take and the decisions they make always be driven by what is in the best interest of the foundation and not of other organizations, causes, populations, or ideologies.

The issue of conflicts of interest is salient because members of a foundation's Board are capable, prominent, and active individuals in their communities, with multiple areas of personal and professional interest and involvement. It is inevitable - indeed expected - that situations will arise in which the board must reach a decision about an organization or activity in which one of its members has an interest that represents an actual, potential, or apparent conflict.

Accordingly, it is important that foundation board members, both as individuals and as a group, adopt standards of conduct and behavior designed to protect the integrity of board decision-making processes, and preserve the quality, fairness, and openness of the foundation's grantmaking development, review, funding, and oversight processes, as well as all its other financial transactions.

POLICY

It is the policy of the foundation to make no grants or other expenditures in a transaction involving a conflict of interests between a board member's obligations to the foundation, his/her interest outside the foundation, or loyalty to another organization – whether for-profit or not-for-profit – unless there is full compliance with procedures established to eliminate or minimize the impact of such a conflict on the foundation's integrity and financial position.

DEFINITIONS

For the purpose of this policy statement, a conflict of interest exists if a board member, or a close relative of a board member, while acting on behalf of himself or herself, or on behalf of some other organization, takes or proposes to take any action that would result in, or give the appearance of resulting in, a financial gain or advantage to that individual, relative, or organization, or would result in an adverse effect on the foundation's integrity or financial position.

In the case of this policy:

- "Organization" shall mean: (i) any business enterprise from which the foundation might purchase goods or services; (ii) any educational, research, policy, healthcare, social service or other nonprofit entity which represents a current or potential future recipient of foundation grant funds; and (iii) any for-profit or not-for-profit entity with which the foundation might partner or collaborate.

- "Acting on behalf of some other organization" shall mean: (i) in the case of nonprofit organizations, serving as a trustee/director, paid staff, advisor, or volunteer, or having a relative who serves one of these functions; and (ii) in the case of for-profit organizations, serving as an owner, director, employee, advisor, counsel, or other capacity, or having a relative who serves one of those capacities, or holding sufficient financial interest as to potentially benefit materially from transactions with the foundation, or having a relative who holds such an interest.

- "Relative" shall mean spouse, life partner, child, grandchild, parent, in-law, or sibling;

- "Financial interest" shall mean: (i) an actual or potential ownership or material investment interest in an entity with which the foundation has a transaction or arrangement; or (ii) a compensation arrangement (direct or indirect remuneration, as well substantial gifts or favors) with the Foundation or with any entity or individual with which the foundation has an actual or potential transaction or arrangement.

IMPLEMENTATION

Effective avoidance of situations that pose a threat to the integrity or financial position of the foundation is the shared responsibility of individual members and of the board as a whole.

The Responsibility of Each Board Member: It is the responsibility of individual board members to be vigilant and sensitive about situations that represent actual, potential, or apparent conflicts between his or her obligation to the foundation and an interest - financial or otherwise - in an external organization or activity. Each member of the board shall:

- Annually deliver to the board chair and to the chief staff officer a completed disclosure form (see model form), supplemented, in writing, as potential conflict situations arise;

- In addition, disclose conflict situations at the time when the board, board committee, or staff is discussing such situations, deliberating their merits, or voting on their disposition; and

- Absent himself or herself from the portion of any board, board committee, or other foundation meeting involving such discussion, deliberation, or voting, making himself or herself available to the board, board committee, or staff to respond to questions.

The Responsibility of the Entire Board: It is the responsibility of the board as a whole to maintain and implement policies and procedures that assure that, at no time, do situations constituting actual, potential, or apparent conflicts of interest in any way jeopardize the integrity and financial position of the foundation. This involves assuring that:

- All transactions between the foundation and external individuals and organizations are based on objective review by disinterested parties;

- Each member complies with foundation policies concerning the disclosure of conflict situations and recusal from deliberations, decisions, and votes;

- Records of board, board committee, and other foundation deliberations, decisions, and votes accurately record the existence of conflict situations and the recusal by the member involved; and

- A policy of strict confidentiality concerning all board, board committee, or other foundation discussions, actions, decisions, and materials is adhered to.

Appendix A: Board Members Conflict of Interest Disclosure Form

The purpose of this form is to identify relationships between foundation board members, or their close relatives, and outside organizations that have the potential to jeopardize the foundation's integrity or financial position. The foundation's conflict of interest policy, along with relevant definitions, responsibilities, and procedures, are spelled out in the attached policy statement.

I. Adherence to the Policy: I understand the foundation's conflict of interest policy and the procedures put in place to implement that policy, and agree to comply with them in good faith.

II. NonProfit Organizations: I, or a close relative as defined in the policy, serve the following nonprofit organizations as a director, trustee, employee, advisor, or volunteer:

Organization	Role in Organization	Signee/Relative

III. For-Profit Organizations: I, or a close relative as defined in the policy, serve the following business enterprises as an owner, director, employee, advisor, counsel, or other capacity, or as a holder of sufficient financial interest as to potentially benefit materially from transactions with the foundation:

Organization	Role in Organization	Signee/Relative

It is understood that full compliance with the foundation's conflict of interest policy requires that: (i) I identify conflict situations at the time of discussion, deliberation, or voting by the board or a board committee; and that (ii) I recuse myself from such discussion (except for answering specific questions about which I have information that may be helpful to my colleagues), deliberation, or voting.

_____   _____
Name/Date   Signature

Appendix B: Conflicts of Interest Policy for Foundation Staff

CONTEXT AND OBLIGATIONS

In considering one's obligations as a member of the staff of a foundation, it is important to understand the special public status of the foundation and its accompanying obligations.

Foundations are accorded the privileges of a public trust, based on the assumption that the foundation will optimize use of its tax-exempt resources in the public's direct interest. The burden of proof is on the foundation to demonstrate that it is meeting this standard and therefore deserves the continuing privileges of their protected status.

As employees of a public trust, staff members are expected to establish and maintain standards of fairness, as well as to meet their specific obligations and responsibilities to the organization. When entering into financial transactions with business enterprises and vendors, the overriding obligation of staff is to protect the foundation's financial position. In distributing foundation resources to the community in the form of grants, the overriding obligation of the staff is to protect the foundation's credibility, integrity, and fairness in dealing with the issues it addresses and the grantee communities and organizations with which it partners. This requires that the actions staff members take and the decisions they make always be driven by what is in the best interest of the foundation and not of other organizations, causes, populations, or ideologies.

The issue of conflicts of interest is salient because members of the foundation's staff are often active individuals in their communities, with multiple areas of personal and professional interest and involvement. It is inevitable - indeed expected - that situations will arise in which the foundation must reach a decision about an organization or activity in which a staff member has an interest that represents an actual, potential, or apparent conflict.

Accordingly, it is important that foundation staff, both as individuals and as a group, adopt standards of conduct and behavior designed to protect the integrity of foundation decision-making processes, and preserve the quality, fairness, and openness of the foundation's grantmaking development, review, funding, and oversight processes, as well as all its other financial transactions.

103

POLICY

It is the policy of the foundation to make no grants or other expenditures in a transaction involving a conflict of interest between a staff member's obligations to the foundation and his/her or interest in, or loyalty to, another organization – whether for-profit or not-for-profit – unless there is full compliance with procedures established to eliminate or minimize the impact of such a conflict on the foundation's integrity and financial position.

DEFINITIONS

For the purpose of this policy statement, a conflict of interest exists if a member of the staff, or a relative of a staff member, while acting on behalf of himself or herself, or on behalf of some other organization, takes or proposes to take any action that would result in, or give the appearance of resulting in, a financial gain or advantage to that individual, relative, or organization, or would result in an adverse effect on the foundation's integrity or financial position.

In the case of this policy:

- "Organization" shall mean: (i) any business enterprise from which the foundation might purchase goods or services; (ii) any educational, research, policy, health care, social service or other non-profit entity which represents a current or potential future recipient of foundation grant funds; and (iii) any for-profit or not-for-profit entity with which the foundation might partner or collaborate.

- "Acting on behalf of some other organization" shall mean: (i) in the case of not-for-profit organizations, serving as a trustee/director, paid staff, advisor, or volunteer, or having a relative who serves one of these functions; and (ii) in the case of for-profit organizations, serving as an owner, director, employee, advisor, counsel, or other capacity, or having a relative who serves one of those capacities, or holding sufficient financial interest as to potentially benefit materially from transactions with the foundation, or having a relative who holds such an interest.

- "Relative" shall mean spouse, life partner, child, parent, in-law, or sibling;

- "Financial interest" shall mean: (i) an actual or potential ownership or other material investment interest in an entity with which the foundation has a transaction or arrangement; or (ii) a compensation arrangement (direct or indirect remuneration, as well substantial gifts or favors) with the foundation or with any entity or individual with which the foundation has an actual or potential transaction or arrangement.

IMPLEMENTATION

Effective avoidance of situations that pose a threat to the integrity or financial position of the foundation is the shared responsibility of individual staff members and of foundation management.

The Responsibility of Each Member of the Staff: It is the responsibility of individual staff to be vigilant and sensitive about situations that represent actual, potential, or apparent conflicts between his or her obligation to the foundation and an interest - financial or otherwise - in an external organization or activity. Each member of the staff shall:

- Annually deliver to the chief staff officer a completed conflict of interest disclosure form (see model form), supplemented, in writing, as potential conflict situations arise;

- In addition, disclose conflict situations at the time when the staff, board, or board committee is discussing such situations, deliberating their merits, preparing recommendations, or voting; and

- Absent himself or herself from the portion of any staff, board, board committee, or other foundation meeting involving such discussion, deliberation, or (in the case of the board or board committee) voting, making himself or herself available to the board, board committee, or staff to respond to questions.

The Responsibility of the Management: It is the responsibility of the foundation's management to maintain and implement policies and procedures that assure that at no time do situations constituting actual, potential, or apparent conflicts of interest in any way jeopardize the integrity and financial position of the foundation. This involves assuring that:

- All transactions between the foundation and external individuals and organizations are based on objective review by disinterested parties;

- Each member of the staff complies with foundation policies concerning the disclosure of conflict situations and recusal from deliberations, decisions, and votes;

- Records of staff, board, and board committee deliberations, decisions, and votes accurately record the existence of conflict situations and the recusal by the staff member involved; and

- A policy of strict confidentiality concerning all staff, board, and board committee discussions, actions, decisions, and materials is adhered to.

Appendix B: Staff Member Conflict of Interest Disclosure Form

The purpose of this form is to identify relationships between foundation staff, or their close relatives, and outside organizations that have the potential to jeopardize the foundation's integrity or financial position. The foundation's conflict of interest policy, along with relevant definitions, responsibilities, and procedures, are spelled out in the attached policy statement.

I. Adherence to the Policy: I understand the foundation's conflict of interest policy and the procedures put in place to implement that policy, and agree to comply with them in good faith.

II. NonProfit Organizations: I, or a close relative as defined in the policy, serve the following nonprofit organizations as a director, trustee, employee, advisor, or volunteer:

Organization	Role in Organization	Signee/Relative

III. For-Profit Organizations: I, or a close relative as defined in the policy, serve the following business enterprises as an owner, director, employee, advisor, counsel, or other capacity, or as a holder of sufficient financial interest as to potentially benefit materially from transactions with the foundation:

Organization	Role in Organization	Signee/Relative

I understand that full compliance with the foundation's conflict of interest policy requires that: (i) I identify conflict situations at the time of discussion, deliberation, or decision by the staff, by the board, or by a board committee; and that (ii) I recuse myself (except for answering specific questions about which I have information that may be helpful to my colleagues) from such discussion, deliberation, or voting.

_____   _____
Name/Date   Signature

About the Author

DENIS J. PRAGER, Ph.D.

Denis J. Prager is president of Strategic Consulting Services, a private consulting practice established in 1994 to help a wide range of organizations think, plan, and act more strategically. Prior to this, he has also worked with the John D. and Catherine T. MacArthur Foundation as Deputy Director and Director of the Foundation's Health Program where he was responsible for the development and implementation of programs in mental health and human development, and in tropical disease research. He has also served as a visiting fellow at the National Academy of Sciences where he established a new, ongoing forum to address problems in the support and conduct of academic research and training.

Dr. Prager has also served as a senior staff member and associate director of the White House Office of Science and Technology Policy where he was responsible for the formulation and implementation of national science and technology policies in the areas of health, agriculture, and environmental sciences.

Dr. Prager began his career in 1960 as a research scientist at the National Institutes of Health (NIH), working on the development of biomedical instrumentation. He also served as a U.S. Public Health Service Fellow at Stanford University in Palo Alto, CA, where he conducted research on the dynamics of the immune system. He subsequently became a branch chief at NIH, directing a program of contract research in reproductive biology and fertility control. From there he moved to the Battelle Memorial Institute, where he was the Director of the Battelle Population Research Center, then associate director of the Battelle Seminars and Studies Program and corporate research fellow.

Dr. Prager received his bachelor's degree in electrical engineering from the University of Cincinnati in Cincinnati, Ohio, and his Ph.D. in physiology from Stanford University in Palo Alto, CA.

He can be reached at pragerd@att.net.